WHERE THE MONSTER Weights

WAITS

WHERE THE MONSTER Weights

HOW ANOREXIA HELD ME HOSTAGE

BY CORINNE WEBER

BALBOA
PRESS

A DIVISION OF HAY HOUSE

Scripture taken from the Holy Bible, NEW INTERNATIONAL VERSION®. Copyright © 1973, 1978, 1984 by Biblica, Inc. All rights reserved worldwide. Used by permission. NEW INTERNATIONAL VERSION® and NIV® are registered trademarks of Biblica, Inc. Use of either trademark for the offering of goods or services requires the prior written consent of Biblica US, Inc.

Author Photo by Nathan Worden | Worden Photography

Balboa Press books may be ordered through booksellers or by contacting:

Balboa Press
A Division of Hay House
1663 Liberty Drive
Bloomington, IN 47403
www.balboapress.com
1 (877) 407-4847

Cover design by Courtney Alberson.
Back cover image © Courtney Alberson, Stacia Hiramine.

Print information available on the last page.

ISBN: 978-1-5043-2940-8 (sc)
ISBN: 978-1-5043-2957-6 (e)

Library of Congress Control Number: 2015903824

Balboa Press rev. date: 04/30/2015

To my brother.
I'm so proud of the person you've become
through the struggles you've endured.
You've come back to me, and I'm forever grateful.

Consider it pure joy, my brothers and sisters, whenever you face trials of many kinds, because you know that the testing of your faith produces perseverance.

—James 1:2–3

Contents

Preface

I knew my life was spinning out of control when, at eighteen years old, I found myself in the baby food aisle at Target. I didn't have a baby. I wasn't pregnant. But what I needed right then could only be found in that section. Frantic and out of time, I fought to look composed in case someone came around the corner.

From the shelf, a cherubic face drew me to a shiny yellow-and-purple package, playfully calling me to choose Gerber Graduates Yogurt Melts in the mixed-berry flavor. A giggle escaped my mouth as I reached out to accept the child's invitation. Then I hesitated and checked myself, glancing up and down the passageway before embracing the answer to my current problem. I wasn't planning on shoplifting, but I sure looked like it.

There I stood like a back-alley addict considering her next fix. Scanning the nutritional panel, I calculated the thirty calories into my daily allotment. I wondered what lie I could tell my mother about why

I'd chosen baby food for a snack. A shiver ran down my spine. I realized the thought had morphed from personal joke to careful consideration. The baby on the package, with its forbidden fruit, became a siren and a muse that day—a telling symbol of my sickness.

Acknowledgments

- God, thank You for showing me how to trust.
- Mr. and Mrs. Olah—two of my high school teachers, who became important mentors in my life during a very dark time. You believed in me and lifted me up when my world collapsed. I will never forget your kindness, love, and the trust you placed in me.
- Shirley Darling—the world's most wonderful, caring college counselor. Thank you for your confidence in me and for introducing me to Chapman University. Without you, Chapman and the people there who helped me recover may well not have been in my life.
- I am grateful to the people of Chapman University for providing a nurturing and fun environment that turns hormonal, whacked-out teenagers into productive and passionate adults. President Doti, thank you for inspiring students to pursue creative excellence—a critical component in my motivation

toward recovery; Becky Konowicz, you welcomed me into my first choice of universities. I am indebted to you—the best admissions officer out there. Jason . . . words can't describe my gratitude.

- My sisters—not only all the amazing members of Gamma Phi Beta, but also all the girls I count as family in many sororities—I now understand why going Greek adds color and depth to college life. Your support, love, and willingness to put up with the annoyances of my illness got me through the rough times.

- Susan and Linda, the dynamic duo, your team effort kept me out of in-house treatment, and looking back, that is a miracle.

- The Editorial Department: Liz Felix (Logistics Coordinator); Jane Ryder (Director of Client Services); Julie Miller (Line Edit); Marcia Ford (Manuscript Annotation). It's a hard thing to have someone advise you to delete large sections of a manuscript. After a time of anger, self-pity, and doubt, clarity comes and the revising continues. Thank you for telling me I had a story that others needed to hear, for encouraging me when I thought about giving up, and for shaping the manuscript into something readable.

- The team at Balboa Press: Thank you for taking me on as a client and for being patient with me as I learned to navigate the publishing process. Heather

Perry, you touched base with me week after week for well over a year. You answered every email and every question in a timely manner. Thank you for going above and beyond my expectations.

- Thank you Laura Jacobus for the final edit. Your positive tone and approach accompanied by your skill in analyzing detail pushed the manuscript over the finish line!
- Mom, thank you for the hours of research and for jogging my memory during the blurry moments.
- Daddy, you loved your little girl unconditionally, and you were always supportive of whatever it took to get me the help I needed. You and I are so much alike, and I never want that to change.

A Note from Daddy

As a father I found this a hard book to read—but it was an even harder story to live. I was there. I saw it, I was part of it, and it happened on my watch. How, as a father, could I have allowed things to go so far, to get so bad, to sneak up on me so quietly and so completely? How could I have failed to protect my daughter—someone I love with all my heart, mind, and soul? How could I have been so blind, so absent, and yet so much there?

Society is obsessed with appearance and suffers an epidemic of apathy or, perhaps, busyness. The media drives our self-images and actions, telling us how we should look, how we should behave, and what will make us feel accepted and happy. We live in isolation—with four iPads at a dinner of four and kids sitting alone for hours at the computer, PSP, or Xbox. This society allows parents to neglect their children, and the lack of attention can be every bit as damaging as physical or mental abuse. We have too often settled into an unthinking apathy.

I never thought I was apathetic. I was active with my children, and when I was in town, I made a point of walking my daughter to school every day. I cheered on the sidelines as she played rugby. I went to the concerts. I was there for our meals. Still, I was detached from the illness creeping into our family. I didn't see it.

I didn't see the shadows form under my daughter's eyes. Instead, for months I saw her with the cheery attitude I wanted to see, even when our family was broken apart by the challenges of teenage life. I was there, but I didn't see the pressure society placed on our kids to drink, to party, and to look (and to be) perfect. I was there, but I didn't see the emotional stress and trauma right in front of me, and for that, I'll forever feel guilty. I was too busy with my own life and explained away what I didn't want to see; I was consumed with my career, addressing the other issues plaguing our family, and pursuing my own passions and interests.

I have learned that many kinds of death can arise from one's omissions just as easily as it can arise from intentional conduct. Realizing I'd been a part of the problem—that I'd almost let death happen in my home because I wasn't aware it was creeping in through the back door—well, a lot of guilt comes with that. And, again, I didn't see it coming. Heck, sometimes I still don't see it. And that scares me.

Anorexia is a hard word to say. It's also a growing trend and has become a huge business for health-care providers. Although I believe most providers are well meaning, the reality is that anorexia is hard to treat, time-consuming to defeat, and (as is the case with most forms of mental illness) incredibly expensive to cure. Many people don't have the financial ability to treat anorexia the way the experts say it should be treated.

I hope that Corinne's story can help other families find ways to fight the disease without taking on huge financial burdens to pay for care that statistics say fails as often as it succeeds. I also hope that others can see from our story that it's possible to treat the disease without in-house care—although I question whether this illness ever completely goes away and don't doubt the necessity of in-house care in some circumstances.

Most of all, it's my profound prayer that this book and our story will provide hope to those who at times feel helpless against a surreptitious stranger—one that has made its home in a child's head right in front of caring parents who simply aren't aware of its presence.

This book is a story of survival. It's a story of family and how love and faith can reverse the death sentence of apathy and ignorance. Above all else, it's a story of hope told by a courageous survivor who I'm fortunate enough to call my daughter. It's her story of strength.

Words can never describe how proud I am of Corinne's mother, Sondra, for sitting up with our daughter for nights on end—counseling her, loving her, and fretting for her. Watching a daughter slowly die before your eyes, every day for months, is horrific, and only those who have lived it can understand the depths of our agony.

Likewise, I can't say enough how grateful I am to the health-care providers who gave their time, energy, and wisdom to Corinne to help her come to grips with this disease. I'm also grateful to God for what we've learned through this experience, for giving me an amazing family, and for showing me how love can combat this condition and how a family can be reborn.

Finally, words can't express how proud I am of my beautiful daughter for having the courage to decide to get well—and then, once that decision was made, to do it. This sounds so silly; after all, who would want to be sick? But that's one of the dangers of this disease: its victims don't look sick; in fact, they look just like the magazines say they should. *Sick* is actually a good word for a society that drives anorexia and its symptoms in pursuit of the almighty dollar.

I hope this story helps parents, especially fathers like myself, know that they're not alone, that others have traveled this road before. I also hope that our journey helps people open their eyes to the consequences of society's values, especially in their own families.

This story is also a call to action for me to be more diligent and observant, particularly since neglect (or worse, apathy) can be the worst form of abuse. However, it is a habit that, with a lot of love, time, and support, can be corrected.

May this book bring you hope and show you a way to recovery.

Ill-Defined

I once heard a doctor on TV say that every anorexia patient he'd seen in his office was a straight-A student. Well, I wasn't a straight-A student. I struggled for every B I ever got. It seems even the experts have a difficult time classifying those of us who starve ourselves.

Anorexia thrives in certain environments. It feeds on perfectionism. And it targets overachievers. But even then, the disease requires "triggers"—negative events usually centered on some tragedy, illness, or insecurity—to develop. And it takes time.

I haven't heard from one person who suffers with anorexia that she, or he, chose to have an eating disorder. We don't one day stumble onto the grand idea of restricting our diet or throwing up after a meal. It's a gradual process. Anorexia invades us then quietly begins its destruction before we know what's hit us. If it isn't caught early, this form of mental illness can be quite dangerous. A killer, in fact.

This killer is smart. It's cunning. And it is patient. When I was first told I had anorexia, I wanted to know everything about it. That seemed only fair because apparently it knew everything about me.

It knew my insecurities, my personality, and my problems. It also had known the exact moment to begin reprogramming my ideas about food—when I was down and desperate. This *it* had been studying me. This thing I would later come to know as my monster first approached me as a friend. It introduced itself as orthorexia.

Orthos means correct or right; *orexis* means appetite. Correct appetite. It must have known I'd Google it. My obsessive-compulsive food and exercise habits had grown increasingly peculiar, even to me. But my subjective research revealed that my food intake placed me in a category well within the healthy range. It confirmed what I thought all along. I just wanted to eat "right." So I had what I thought was a correct appetite. That comforted me. And it sounded perfectly reasonable. After all, the subtle changes in my diet were meant for good, focused on nutrition and bettering myself.

I come from a family that enjoys the outdoors and exercise. When I was growing up, healthy eating was important, but not excessively so. I remember helping my mother make chicken soup, a southern favorite. She kept cut-up carrots and bowls of grapes in the fridge, but we also had pizza nights followed with Blue Bell ice cream.

But I have to remember that anorexia is not just about food—not at its core, anyway. That's why the disease is so confusing. From the outside, it may look like someone with anorexia obsesses about food and weight and that's all there is to it—that anorexia is a body-image problem that can be solved once the celebrity wannabe realizes life's not all about looks. The correction in body image will allow the misguided victim to stop the nonsense, eat like a normal person, and enjoy it.

Problem is, being able to eat and enjoy it is an illusion for the anorexic. This form of mental illness is not about ego. Those of us who live with anorexia are trying to find ways to cope in a world that is spinning out of our control.

Many of us fail: anorexia is the number-one killer of those with mental illness (including those who have depression). And those of us who do recover are left with permanent scars. Even after treatment and even after being in recovery, I find anorexic thoughts can still surface in times of stress. I've been told that in time my monster may leave and never return. That gives me hope. But for now, its voice is still there. My monster lurks in the corner of my mind and sometimes begs for attention, sounding like an old friend who offers help and intimacy. But I now know that "old friend" is full of deceit and even death. That's the power of recovery. I have the choice not to listen to the lie inside my mind. My monster no longer rules over me.

Some of you may think you wouldn't fall into an eating disorder given similar circumstances. Eating disorders are for weak-minded people, right? On the contrary, anorexics can be determined and quite methodical. How else could we deny ourselves the very things we desperately long for? Or calculate the calories processed in and out of our bodies?

You may also think that those with an eating disorder decide to restrict or to purge, so we should then be able to decide to stop. Not so. After a certain point (usually after too much time has passed), the disease takes on a life of its own.

People ask me how it all started. I can tell you the exact moment anorexia entered my life: high school, fall semester of my junior year. But the series of triggers that led up to that event—those might have begun before I was born.

Slung to Singapore

My brother and I played together even before birth, tossing and turning inside my mother. I'm told he came out first, winning over the nurses' hearts with his blue eyes and his curly brown hair. I, however, was not ready. I turned and braced my legs against my mother's pelvis and fought for twenty-six minutes to remain as close to her as possible. Anxiety and worry were part of my genetic makeup.

Yes, I think I've always been an anxious girl. Cautious. Thoughtful about my choices. My brother is the exact opposite. He's the impulsive one, ready to try anything that, to my mind, seems a bit dangerous.

When we were young, whenever my brother got in trouble with Mom and Dad, I'd ask to take his punishment. He couldn't stand to be in time-out, and I wanted to save him. He, in turn, wanted to save me from imaginary fire-breathing dragons on the playground. Corbin was my best friend, and I was his.

Our friendship deepened after a job opportunity for my father uprooted our family from our home in Dallas and sent us to Singapore, a tropical financial hub one degree north of the equator in Southeast Asia. I remember Dad's demeanor when he delivered the news—it gave me a glimpse of what he might have looked like as a small boy just before opening presents on Christmas morning. His memory of the best gift he'd ever opened on that special day would have been hard to match what he'd been given as a thirty-six-year-old man—the chance to follow his father's international footsteps—and seeing the look on his face, we couldn't say no.

So at eight years old, Corbin and I had said good-bye to the only life we'd known: the live oaks dotting our front lawn, a neighborhood swimming pool across the street, family, friends, three dogs, a red Suburban, and donuts picked up at the drive-through Sunday mornings before church.

Learning the Asian culture overwhelmed my brother and me at first, but it also solidified our bond. We observed our parents morph into some hybrid race as they attempted to immerse themselves in local customs. One night at dinner Mom ate a fish eyeball, casually chewing and commenting on its flavor. I responded by throwing up on a nearby bush. Finished with the experiment of living abroad, I announced my desire to return home to Dallas. My parents must have realized Corbin and I were having a hard time adjusting, because they began chatting about a possible family addition that excited all four of us.

Scooter's adoption was my parents' answer to our hesitation over a long-term stay in Singapore. Sometimes a dog is all you need. After that, it didn't take long for us to settle into a life that reflected the normalcy we'd known in Texas. Soccer practice. Music lessons. Church. There were even donuts, although not as sweet and sometimes topped with pork floss.

Two years passed quickly. Peculiar how easy it is to assimilate into a surrounding environment. Lunch every Sunday after church now included an order of cheese naan and tandoori chicken. While ordering, we'd even make a go at Singlish, a local slang concoction consisting of English, Mandarin, and Malay. At least we were trying. Instead of answering the waiter with a "yes" or a "no," we now replied with "*can*" or "*cannot*." And, in striking up further conversation, we'd force a "*lah*" at the end of, well, too many sentences. The added syllable was meant for emphasis, but our enthusiasm only revealed our newbie status on the island.

Okay-lah! symbolized our lives balancing between two worlds—Singapore and our home country.

Corbin and I enjoyed the entire year of sixth grade. We spent much of our free time together, walking to a friend's house to swim or to our American school to shoot baskets. We shared a lot of friends then. But at the end of that school year, Corbin's close friends moved back to the States. I still had girlfriends for sleepovers and shopping, but Corbin was left to start over in search of a good buddy.

A boy from a military background filled in the gap. An outgoing guy with a friendly disposition, John would come over and greet my parents with a big smile, sometimes reserving a hug for Mom. He and my brother would then find something to do. The two became inseparable during seventh grade, spending almost every day together.

That year, I watched Corbin take on a different personality. He became distant and spent more time in his room. His off-campus wardrobe transformed into all things dark: black shirts, black pants, black shoes, black socks. He even wore Polo Black cologne. He let his hair grow out. I wondered what mysterious goth-like creature hid behind the fringe. I caught the stale smell of smoke when he walked by me.

All that said, at school Corbin seemed fine. He sat with friends in the lunchroom. He played on the football team and participated in scouting. When the principal pulled him aside for a uniform violation, Corbin smiled and dutifully tucked in his shirt. He was a likable and cheerful guy.

Until Jackie. At first, the idea of Corbin having a girlfriend troubled Mom. She wanted us to wait at least until high school before dating. But she softened her stance when she found out that Jackie's mother held an officer position for the US Embassy and that her retired father reportedly once had associations with Oliver North and Ronald Reagan. So Corbin and Jackie became an item. But Jackie came across as a little too flirtatious and seemed to have an eye for John.

By the end of seventh grade, slight scratch marks appeared on my brother's wrists. I didn't know what they were; when I asked, he'd act offended and stalk off to his room. One afternoon, I overheard my mother ask him about something I hadn't seen.

"Corbin, what in the world is on your arms?" Mom sounded more quizzical than concerned.

"John challenged me in a dare," my brother said, without looking at her.

"What do you mean *dare*?" She took a closer look at the raw and irritated circular marks on the undersides of both my brother's forearms and sounded more worried.

"It's just a game, Mom."

Corbin's attempts to reassure her didn't work. She continued pressing until he fessed up.

"We put our forearms together and hold them there while one of us drops a cigarette. Whoever pulls away first is the loser."

No one, especially Corbin, wanted to be a loser.

Shouting matches erupted between he and his girlfriend. I'd ask him if he wanted to talk, but he'd shut me out. Hurt and confused, I started obsessing about our relationship. I thought I must have done something to make Corbin avoid me. I wondered if I annoyed him. I needed him to like me; he was my brother, after all, and even more than that, my twin. We were supposed to be connected—always.

Toward the middle of eighth grade, Mom noticed the strain in our relationship. She advised me to give it some time. But the saying that time heals doesn't always apply. Over the months that followed, Corbin's rebellion waxed, and my confidence waned. Mom attempted to soothe my festering emotional wounds by reminding me to pull my shoulders back and stand up straight. "It'll make you feel better, sweetheart," she said.

I wasn't myself around my friends either. I'd still go for sleepovers and movie dates—and had many fun moments—but I never felt at ease. Insecurity caused me to second-guess things I said. I wondered if I fit in. I'd make up excuses for why I needed to go home.

School was no better. Corbin began making fun of me. He called me an idiot in front of his friends. He resisted my hugs. I'd put my head down and walk away, trying to imagine a world where I mattered.

I didn't know it then, but I had created within myself an environment where anorexia could thrive:

redirecting my thoughts in times of stress, making myself numb through distraction, avoiding feelings. But at the time, I saw no other way.

High school expanded students' opportunities to become independent. The course offerings, club choices, and travel teams kept my mind busy with goals and aspirations. I stayed away from Corbin and accepted that siblings don't always get along. I got a cat.

Animals had always been a passion of mine, and as students began fine-tuning their hobbies and interests, I gravitated toward helping creatures in need. The worthy cause spawned an idea. I set out to start a club and found a teacher to sponsor the project, partnering the school with an established no-kill shelter for dogs. Puppy Love became my purpose. I know. Cheesy name. But it got the point across. And people joined. Students enjoyed the hands-on interaction as they resocialized abused and abandoned dogs for future adoption into loving families. At times, I would entertain the idea that I was one of those dogs—one of the lucky ones. What would it be like to have someone come to the rescue and offer a brand new start—a second chance for a life of love and acceptance?

Between the growing club and playing rugby, my free time was fully booked, allowing much-needed space between my brother and me.

Corbin seemed to enjoy the change in environment as well. Jackie and John had moved away, giving Corbin yet another chance to redefine himself. He cut his hair. He joined the high school football team and, selected to play varsity as a freshman, he attracted attention from the upperclassmen, widening his social circle.

My brother was one of those guys who could pull off a tough persona on the field—playing linebacker at a stocky 215 pounds built more on muscle than on fat—then change into his Boy Scout uniform and run from practice to troop meeting. But trying to balance these two roles and their expectations would prove difficult.

One night while walking down Orchard Road, Corbin felt a tap on his shoulder. He turned to see two seniors. "Come on," one of them said. "We're going to Newton." This invitation to visit the popular local hawker center—an outdoor food court, Singapore style—and sit with the upcoming graduates offered a much better alternative to the game arcade. Corbin wasn't about to turn them down.

Breaking the eleven o'clock curfew had consequences. We usually needed special permission for passing curfew. Corbin had no legitimate reason to be out late that night. Knowing our parents would catch on to his telltale slurring if he called with some made-up excuse for an extension, he called me instead.

"Corinne, I spent my taxi money. Can you pick me up on your way home?"

I could imagine my parents busting my brother when he walked into the house asking for taxi fare. They'd smell the alcohol. It wouldn't be pretty. Disappointed Mom would deliver a lecture. Dad would wake him up early for a dose of mountain biking in the jungle as punishment. My protective instincts kicked in.

"Where are you?" I asked.

"I'm at Newton. Meet me at the taxi stand."

"The movie just let out so the taxi queue's kinda long. I'll be there in fifteen minutes," I said.

Corbin sometimes drank but not like that, especially not when a mandatory parental greet-and-sniff awaited him at home. He climbed into the taxi, bringing the smell of alcohol with him. He said he'd had a pint of Tiger Beer and then thought he should leave. But when he made a move to go, the guys placed another pint in front of him and said, "There's your exit pass." Corbin chugged the beer and set down the empty glass with a senior-size burp. The guys cheered, and Corbin left, knowing he had no money and only minutes before the effects would show up as evidence.

I swore under my breath. How could I cover this up with Mom and Dad? I didn't even consider that Corbin's mess-up shouldn't become my problem; I was his twin and therefore responsible to make it all okay.

I called Mom's cell. She picked up on the first ring.

"Hi Corinne. Dad and I are out walking by the river at Clark Quay. We should be home within the hour."

Perfect.

"Oh, great! Glad you and Daddy are having fun. Corby's with me. We're almost home and we're really tired. Can you wake me up in the morning? I have to be at a car wash for Puppy Love."

When I hung up, I'd regained hero status with my brother. He snuggled up against me in the taxi.

I'd enjoy the attention as long as it would last. But Corbin's skyrocketing popularity with the older guys didn't help our relationship, especially seeing as restaurants still offered me the kids' menu. He was definitely the older one, and all twenty-eight minutes of that difference showed up in every area of our lives.

The second year of high school arrived quicker than expected. Sophomores walked with increased confidence up the high school steps and through the halls, having passed down the freshman dos and don'ts to a new class of students. We knew where to sit in the cafeteria and where our groups hung out. We also knew where not to go. Seniors occupied the upstairs lunchroom tables next to Subway, an area definitely off limits to underclassmen.

Older, wiser, and more prepared, we relaxed a little on the social side and turned our attention to making something of ourselves. At the time, I wanted to be a veterinarian—or at least an advocate for animals if my math and science grades failed to align with my dream job. As the day of the Student Council Club Fair approached, I thought about the shelter and the change I'd witnessed in the dogs' personalities—each visit revealed a little less shaking and a little more playing. I created a slideshow to showcase the efforts of a volunteer and the effects they had on the life of a dog. I aimed for ten recruits; more than forty-five attended the first meeting. It would be a busy year managing Puppy Love, rugby, and academics.

Corbin started off the school year strong, holding his own academically, motivated by the coaches' expectations for the travel team. That year the Singapore Falcons planned to compete against an American-school team located in Japan. Corbin did not want to miss out on that November game or on visiting Japan.

He also busied himself with his Eagle Scout project. Sourcing materials and calculating expenses took a lot of time, but Corbin seemed to thrive on the challenge and activity. On occasion, our family of four would gather on the couch and laugh while watching an episode of *Everybody Loves Raymond*. That October Corbin and I celebrated our sweet sixteen. I thought my wish of getting along had come true.

The Falcons won that November game. My brother returned on a high note and ready to celebrate. His friends planned a party for the following Saturday night. Mom and Dad gave special permission for Corbin to stay out late. On the night of the party he called home and asked for a third curfew extension. This time the answer was no—"Nothing good happens after 1 a.m." Corbin threw a fit and hung up.

The three of us were sitting on the couch, catching up on my night out and watching Corbin's plays from a recording of the game when my brother came home. He didn't say a word but walked directly to the bathroom and slammed the door. Mom and I called it a night and went upstairs, giving Dad the opportunity to talk with Corbin.

The next morning I came downstairs at the usual time to leave for church. Sundays were always reserved for church followed by lunch. But Corbin and Dad weren't going. I could tell by the way Dad was dressed, or really by the way he wasn't. He and Corbin sat at the dining room table. I looked at Mom. Her handbag dangled under her shoulder. She signaled me to follow her.

Something was wrong. I tried to make sense of the situation without speaking—experience had shown that fewer words were sometimes best. On my brother's left arm, a trail of dried blood led to a gash that looked like it required stitches. I couldn't tell how far across the cut went; his black T-shirt covered the extent of his injury. Then I noticed a bloodied shark tooth displayed on the table in front of him. Realizing what he'd done, I looked away. The light scratch marks I'd first noticed at the end of seventh grade had progressed into a much deeper problem.

Mom and Dad arranged for family counseling. At the few sessions I attended, I'd listen to my brother rant about not feeling "heard." He said he was so depressed he couldn't focus. He'd shake his fingers toward my parents and accuse them of loving me, the "perfect" one, more. News to me. I thought I was the annoying one. And loving me more? Then why was he getting all the attention?

I didn't see the point in telling my side of the story. Anything to do with me would only aggravate the situation. I sat there … and thought of my cat. I imagined Samson out on my balcony, sitting on my wicker lounge and watching a bird flittering around the pink bougainvillea bushes.

The counselor asked if I had anything to add. I didn't. I'd already decided I didn't want anything to do with my brother. But I also felt pity for my parents. I could tell they were hurting. I struggled for ideas about how to make their lives better—and how to make them stop fighting over what to do about Corbin. I didn't need a counselor for that.

Late one night, I came downstairs for a glass of water. I turned on the light and found my mother sleeping on the marble-tiled floor next to my brother's room. The palm of her hand rested on his bedroom door. I wondered if that was where she prayed for him. I'd seen my father pray over my brother's bed— sometimes he'd even kneel there and whimper.

The following day my mother mentioned she might go away for a while. I knew she was scared of what Corbin might do. I was scared of what he'd do, too, and honestly I was a little scared *of* him. I thought if only I could do better in school or be a better daughter, maybe then my parents would be okay.

Thumb Wars

Mom stayed. I imagined she stayed because of me. Her longer hugs backed up my assumptions. But part of me thought Christmas had changed her mind. The season made her giddy—the lights, the sounds, the anticipation. She occupied her days buying gifts and kept her nights free for me. We'd pass the time together in the kitchen making fudge for teachers' gifts or cookies for the neighbors. Just a few days more and our family would head home to the States.

"Mom!"

I burst into the house, waving my latest exam results. Ninety-two. Bam! Honor roll again. Mom would be thrilled. I came around the corner to see Mom and Corbin at the dining room table.

"Mom, I made honor roll!"

She frowned at me and opened her mouth. She then raised her eyebrows and hands at the same time. Corbin got up from the table, walked to his room, and slammed the door. Shocked, I ran upstairs, threw the papers across my floor, and collapsed on my bed.

I started crying. *What did I do wrong? I made honor roll! What the heck? Really?*

Mom came in.

"Hi, sweetheart. I'm sorry. I'm so sorry. I'm so proud of you."

"Mom, why? Why would you do that?"

"I know. I know. You're doing great. You're trying so hard. And I am … I'm so proud of you. Not just for your grades. For you! I'm proud of you, the person you are. It's just that your accomplishments make Corbin feel terrible. And he's going through a really tough time right now. So when you came in yelling about honor roll in front of him, I … It was just bad timing. Honey, do you understand?"

"I'm sorry, Momma. I know things are hard. I should have thought about Corby."

I thought making the honor roll would change things; lighten my mother's burden. But all I did was add to it.

Christmas break in Colorado came as a welcome relief. Corbin's mood elevated. I guess the mountains and Grandpa lifted his spirits. I spent the mornings and afternoons with Mom. Grandpa, Corbin, and Dad hit the slopes. At night we'd all gather for dinner and talk about our day.

When the time came to leave, Mom flew to Texas. She needed time with her mother. The rest of our family returned to Singapore to prepare for the second semester. I determined to remain as quiet as possible, to focus on my studies and Puppy Love, and to stay away from Corbin.

January in Singapore is mundane only if you're discussing the weather. Constant humidity and ninety-degree days give no indication that the most important Chinese holiday arrives in a few weeks. To sense the excitement in the air, I tune in to the taxi drivers. As Chinese New Year approaches, they play catchy songs on their car radios and are more jovial than usual. The mood is infectious.

The first day of second semester, I took a taxi to school. It looked like rain, and I didn't want to risk getting wet. The driver of the taxi, an old uncle (in Singaporean culture, a younger person will address an older man as "uncle"), sang along with the radio while tapping his hands on the steering wheel. I absorbed his optimism. I thought, *I'm on a roll. If this is what the real world offers, I'm ready.* The feeling mirrored what I felt on a rugby field. I couldn't wait to play again, especially against the Australian school. They didn't have a girls' team, so the boys had to play us. I enjoyed our last match; they had underestimated our competitive nature. I reviewed the plays I'd made, taking advantage of my relative smallness and scooting around them in wing position.

Playing rugby against the Aussies (before I got sick).

The first warning bell rang, jolting me from my daydream. My mind had shifted to autopilot while paying the driver and navigating my way up the steps. *Focus. Five minutes to get to class.* I looked down at my spring schedule that I'd printed off the night before. First period: English with A. Hallam. As I walked up the stairs, I wondered who else would be there. I arrived at the solid blue door labeled "Room 312" and paused. Taking a deep breath, I gripped the crisp metallic handle, anticipating new and old friends and a fun teacher. I didn't know Room 312 would soon gift me with so much more than friends and fun.

I filed in with two other students and immediately felt the warmth of familiarity. Phil was there. Philip Anderson could fill a room with his presence and make any day brighter with his big bear hugs. David Wong stood next to him. I enjoyed looking at David—his smile, his spiked, fine black hair, and the optimistic twinkle in his dark eyes. David was the first guy friend I made in Singapore. I'd seen him around church with his grandma until one day we finally met in Sunday school. I came to call him my brother. His reassuring words would calm me before some quiz or test.

Standing not too far from David was Hayes. I'd once had a crush on him, but his reputation with the girls kept my heart at bay. I took the seat next to David's and asked about his winter break.

Suddenly, the classroom door swung open and an unfamiliar face appeared. I could no longer hear David; my body suspended all other senses to focus my vision. I was mesmerized. A handsome distraction had entered the room. I suddenly remembered seeing him once before at an event for another school club I belonged to. That particular club, Peer Support, familiarized students with the campus and made them feel welcomed into the Singapore American School (SAS) community.

This guy had broad shoulders, and the creases of his shirt outlined his muscles. He stood confidently with a sense of independence. His jawline was strong and attractive. He wore his dark-brown hair a bit longer than I liked, but perfectly combed. He was not only captivating but he looked like the prince I'd dreamed about as a little girl—twirling around in my powder-blue satin dress, a silver plastic crown upon my head, pretending I was as kind as Cinderella and as fair as Snow White. As I shook off my trance, I decided today was a good day for a Disney movie.

Most girls my age no longer dreamed in animation; they'd pushed aside those childish delusions. I still believed in fairy tales, my imagination favoring happy ever afters over prime-time drama series. That day my English class transformed into King Arthur's court, and the predestined prince and/or knight in shining armor took his rightful seat at a desk toward the front of the room. He had me spellbound. Classroom discussion would soon reveal his name: Curtis Alexander.

"Corinne!"

David caught me gazing. He knew me too well.

Mom returned from the States the following week. The thrill of seeing her took a back seat to her immediate line of questioning over the new guy. My comments about Curtis had been brief, but she must have sensed from my tone that I had a crush. Mom's intuition never fails.

English class became the highlight of my day. The class was challenging and the teacher inspiring, but so was the idea of love at first sight being more than a cliché. Curtis and I quickly hit it off and became friends. Besides his physical strength, I sensed an appealing steadfastness in Curtis—an assuredness I longed for. I soon learned he had created his own study-abroad program, bravely leaving his family and the comforts of Colorado to travel overseas and stay with his aunt and uncle, who were teachers at our school. He would be in Singapore for only one semester.

I pulled back from the thought of anything long term, but after a while, a feeling I'd never known surfaced within me. I didn't understand why every time I saw Curtis my palms became wet and my body trembled. I couldn't quiet the small whisper inside telling me he was different.

It was uncanny how much we had in common. We seemed to understand each other in ways most people couldn't comprehend. We shared a pensive quality. We longed for depth and meaning. Curtis and I were also both a bit mischievous. We'd sneak up to the fourth floor of the school during our sixty-minute free periods and steal onto the deserted tennis courts. Sitting on the warm concrete with the sun hitting our backs, we talked about life—our deepest dreams and desires and what we wanted most from ourselves and from others.

As we talked, we found that our lives had followed eerily similar paths. The connections were too numerous to be mere happenstance. He was from

Colorado. I called Colorado home. He had younger twin sisters; I was a twin. Our dads had worked for the same company; they'd even been in the same fraternity. We learned that our maternal grandfathers had died in the same way.

We were dumbstruck.

My feelings grew so strong for Curtis that it became difficult not to be obvious. I'd stared at him during class. I wanted to be with him every second. And one day in the cafeteria, David called me out on it.

"Corinne, you're in love with him!"

"I am not!"

I guess I'd protested too much. David pulled me aside to a secluded area.

"Okay, Okay! Yes, I have feelings for Curtis," I said.

I shied away from David's searching eyes, but he embraced me, signaling his approval. His gesture meant everything to me.

One Friday night while Curtis and I were Skyping, I checked the upper-right corner of my computer screen. The clock read 1:53 a.m. Had we been talking for almost three hours? Neither of us seemed tired. We were too caught up enjoying the conversation to notice something as trivial as fatigue.

"Let's play a game," he said.

"What kind of game?" I asked, the words sounding more flirtatious than I intended.

"How about truth or dare?"

I hesitated. What quest was he on? I agreed to play along. After a few rounds, Curtis asked the one question I'd been dreading.

"Corinne, how do you feel about me?"

He peered into the camera. My heart dropped. Should I tell him? How would he take it?

"Honestly?" My voice quivered.

"Yes," he replied. He sounded calm.

"Curtis, I have feelings for you."

I looked away and then back to the camera to deliver the message I'd desperately wanted him to hear.

"You're unlike any guy I've ever met. You're kind, sweet, good-looking, and I …"

I'd committed. Too late to change course and offer "just kidding" as a cover.

"… I've had a crush on you for the longest time, and I'd love to be able to see you as more than a friend."

Way too late to retrieve the ramblings of an impassioned schoolgirl. I averted my eyes to inspect my fingers. I took note of a slight cuticle tear. I didn't want to look at him, but I fought my cowardice. I turned back to the camera, hopeful. My heart was pounding. Time stopped. A long silence followed. I sensed him struggling. Or maybe I'd boxed him into a corner. What was he thinking?

Finally, Curtis spoke.

"Corinne, you are such a sweet girl, but …"

Oh no. Oh God, why? His words wrenched at my heart.

"… but, I don't think this can work."

My eyes darted back to my hands.

"I'm only here for a semester and then I go back to the States. I can't get invested in a relationship, so … I think it would be best to just be friends."

His words trailed off as meaningless whispers. My hands—something more permanently affixed to me—had won over my attention. My thumbs vied in a self-imposed war, repetitive nail strikes distracting me from despair. I became the referee, blocking out the emotion of the moment. *Left thumb ahead by two.* I realized I needed to offer some sort of reply, but it had to be short.

"It's okay. I understand."

I couldn't force my eyes to return to the camera; they were too busy watching the high-stakes contest between my thumbs. I was ashamed. *I should've known.* Feigning exhaustion, I ended the conversation and went to bed feeling empty and more alone than ever.

I woke up in the morning, crushed, but it wasn't in my nature to give up easily. I'd continue as Curtis' close friend—with the idea that maybe he'd someday realize he wanted more.

One afternoon as I sat at our regular lunch table, listening to the latest gossip, something said in passing made me nauseous. It was about Curtis and a girl he'd hooked up with over the weekend. Apparently it was just a kiss, but he'd never shown that kind of interest in me. I realized my feelings for Curtis had been a waste of time. My heart sank. I got up from the table.

"I have to go." The sternness in my voice surprised me.

David's eyes caught mine as I turned to leave. He knew I was hurt.

Baked Goods and Blood

After Curtis, I realigned my vision, shifting my focus from boys to brain matter. I boycotted animated movies. Who needed a prince anyway? Puppy Love and schoolwork occupied most of my time, and I found fulfillment in both. Seeing a shy, trembling mutt transformed into a playful, trusting potential pet motivated me. I could count on this happy ending. I determined to build a strong foundation to leave as a legacy for those who would run Puppy Love after I left. That said, managing club members proved arduous.

One day at lunch, I read a text on my phone from a volunteer.

"Corinne, there's a problem. No one's at the Puppy Love table."

I received her notice twenty minutes into the lunch period on the day of our biggest bake sale. I panicked.

Sure enough, our donated baked goods lay neglected, piled in a classroom. The two people who signed-up to sell the items during lunch were nowhere around, and they weren't answering my calls. I scrambled to sell what I could and gave away the rest.

I couldn't stop thinking about the missed opportunity to raise money for the dogs—precious dollars that would have helped run the shelter, provide medicine, and supply food.

Instead of sticking around after school to write e-mails and vent to our club sponsor, I decided to go home earlier than usual. For several months, I'd been coming home late to avoid the deepening rift separating our family. But on the day of the bake sale gone bad, I wanted to be home. I wanted to be on my bed, in my bedroom. I'd clear my head and write in my journal. But first I had to relieve a full bladder.

I opened the front door and entered the hallway. Complete silence. No one home. For once I had the whole house to myself. I stole through the living room and headed for the bathroom. Dropping my backpack on the dining-room table, I whipped up my shirt to get at the elastic band on my skirt while dodging my brother's open bedroom door. The familiar sour aroma of sweat and blue Axe body spray wafted through the air as I passed.

I thrust open the slightly ajar bathroom door, intending to finish my business quickly. But as I opened the door, I froze. There was blood on the floor. And in the sink.

I immediately forgot why I was in the bathroom. I checked my brother's room. He wasn't there. I looked in the bathroom again and noticed a towel on the floor, also covered with blood. A small paring knife rested in the sink.

Corbin had been cutting himself a lot more lately. Traces of red on his white uniform shirtsleeves gave that away. But I'd never witnessed firsthand evidence. This time he'd either been in a hurry or he no longer cared about hiding his dark practice. I looked again at the towel, hoping the stains would reveal what my brother was feeling when he cut. Was it pain or relief? Or both?

I turned back toward the living room. Our family portrait hung on the far wall: the four of us happily posed in a tranquil rain-forest setting. My body went numb. I fell to my knees. We were no longer that family, the one I grew up in. The laughter, the closeness, the normalcy—they'd been replaced with tension and distance.

How bad could the cutting get? Could Corbin impulsively cut in the wrong place and bleed out? Would he someday reach his limit and leave me here, half a twin? Could that have happened today? My heart sank as my thoughts raced, wondering where my brother could be. I struggled to the phone and managed to dial my mother. I told her what had happened.

"I'll be right there. Give me forty-five minutes," she said, sounding businesslike.

"Mom, I'm not okay."

"Corinne, you're okay. I'll be right there."

I hung up the phone then curled up in a fetal position on the cold tile floor. My body trembled. *I'm not okay.* I started hyperventilating. I had to get help—or get a hold of myself. Forcing myself to stand, I lumbered to the kitchen, grabbed a plastic bag, and breathed.

By focusing on the rhythmic rising and falling of my chest, I finally calmed down enough to pour myself a glass of water and sit at the dining room table where I waited for my mother. I passed the time calling up childhood memories of my brother, mourning our simpler life of Legos and make-believe.

The sound of the front door opening startled me. I looked up, expecting my mother. It was Corbin. He sauntered in as if nothing had happened. Only modest red stains on his upper-left shirtsleeve revealed anything amiss. He seemed fine. He passed as if I weren't there.

What is wrong with me? I thought I must be going crazy and acting overly dramatic. Corbin was living what seemed to be a normal life—with the exception of self-made slash marks that he sported like badges of honor. I was the one falling apart. His self-harm seemed to make him feel better, but it was driving me mad.

I'd called Mom and blown his cover, and I'd suffer for it. It was one thing to have my brother mad at me, but another to be completely ignored. The person who'd once been my closest friend had become a complete stranger. Tense words escalated into horrible fights and more slammed doors. Family discussions and nurturing became divided by gender. Dad began spending more time with Corbin, taking him on early Saturday morning bike rides. I began avoiding the couch where we'd played Xbox—Dad had taken it over for counseling sessions, calmly espousing words of wisdom to Corbin while the two of them watched *Everybody Loves Raymond*.

I could avoid Corbin at home, but not the bullying beyond our doors—mainly the scoffing at school. I came to expect him to make fun of me in front of his friends. No longer assured of a brother who'd protect me, I began to fear him. I stopped talking when he was around. I didn't want to say something that might invite sarcasm or snide remarks. I stopped expressing my opinions. In fact, I stopped having them. Opinions could cause conflict, and I didn't want the anxiety that came with conflict.

Insecurity spilled into my friendships as well. I found it difficult to make decisions about where to go or what to do with anyone. I'd usually wait to be called. I'd then wait for others to decide what they wanted to do. Only then would I open my mouth in agreement. It didn't matter to me anyway. Nothing did—except I wanted people to stay in my life. But I didn't know how to make that happen, and that scared me. I tried not to burden anyone, even in the smallest of ways. I walked on eggshells. That seemed the logical answer.

At the same time, Curtis invested more in our "friendship." He talked to me on MSN chat and texted me, wondering why I no longer sat at our regular lunch table. I responded to him in a guarded but polite manner, just as I would have to anyone.

As my sophomore year drew to a close I received an invitation to a going away party for Curtis. I wondered if I should make the effort, but I didn't want unpleasant feelings between us. I decided there could be no harm in wishing him well. What could happen? He was leaving. I would never see him again. Simple as that. I mustered up some courage and called my best friend and asked her to go with me.

Angela Kim—beautiful, talented, smart, Korean. She had an eye for art and loved to dance. When my mother said I could invite three girls to Phuket for my sweet sixteen celebration, she was one of them. Unaffected by life, Angela tossed aside problems as temporary annoyances. She viewed each day as something fun and positive. She also loved to eat, although you'd never guess it. Her body could make anyone envious. Some of my favorite memories of us include baking cookies in my kitchen. I called her Donut.

Angela and I approached Curtis' gate in a bright yellow CityCab. We'd been laughing and joking, but as we grabbed our purses, I noticed my hands were clammy. Dressed in a long, sunflower-colored shirt, tight, dark-blue jeans, and black high-heeled shoes, I wanted to make sure I looked good for this final farewell. People were playing beer pong in the front yard. I stepped out of the cab and heard a friendly voice.

"Corinne!"

It was Kathryn, a good friend who'd always been easy to talk to. She was the one who'd mentioned Curtis and his hook-up.

She ran out past the gate and gave me a desperately needed hug. I welcomed the encouragement. Kathryn calmed my fears and my trembling hands as she held me. I pulled back from her embrace and saw Curtis standing behind her. I stood firm. This was the first time I'd seen him in more than two weeks. He looked handsome and strong. His hair was cut short the way I liked it. I could tell by the smooth skin on his jawline that he'd recently shaved.

"Corinne … hi. You look beautiful," he said.

His words permeated my skin, their warmth awakening butterflies in my stomach. *No!* I thought to myself. *You're supposed to be mad at him—remember?*

"Hi, Curtis," I replied.

What I meant was *bye*. A spark of strength and independence began rebuilding my morale. I subdued the faint tickling of fluttering wings then wrapped my own around Donut. We went inside.

As the night wore on, a drinking game began. It was one I'd never played before—king's cup, I believe. I could tell the alcohol was starting to affect me—and Curtis. I caught him looking my way now and then, and one time I even held his gaze for a moment or two. He found ways to talk to me and to sit next to me. I didn't know what to make of this, and decided I needed some space.

"Curtis, do you mind if I borrow your computer for a sec? I need to check something on Facebook."

"Sure," he said. "It's in my room." I was nervous about going into his room, but I needed time to think. As I started to shut the door, a hand wedged its way between the frame and my privacy.

"Can I come in?" Curtis asked.

I opened the door and looked at him, puzzled.

"Of course. It's your room."

Reaching for his laptop, I sat on the middle of the bed and signed into my account, but it was only for show. I couldn't help myself. I stole glances of Curtis while he made himself comfortable, spreading out across the bed and laying his head on my arm.

"I'm *so glad* I met you," he whisper-slurred. "You're unlike any girl I've ever met, and I'm so happy we're friends. What am I gonna do without you?" His lips gently brushed my skin.

I didn't say a word. I couldn't gather my thoughts. Every ticking second echoed. I could hear the sounds of his breathing.

He started lightly kissing my arm. I remained completely still. *Stay in control, Corinne.* My mind raised his lips up my arm, my shoulder, my neck, my chin. I snapped out of my reverie.

Somehow I had placed the laptop by my side. Curtis lingered over me. His thumb rested on my chin, gently tilting it upward so my eyes met his. Then I remembered.

"What the hell are you doing?" I demanded, pushing him off of me. He looked astonished.

"What do you mean?" He cowered behind his amber-colored eyes.

"Exactly what it sounds like. What are you doing? You think you can blow me off then make a move like this before you leave? I'm not that kind of girl—and if you think I am, you have another thing coming."

Curtis stared at me for a long time.

"I didn't know what to do. I was leaving, and even though I had feelings for you, I knew it would be painful to lose you. But I guess that happened anyway."

What? How much time had we lost? How long had he felt this way? I hadn't expected this. I had no rehearsed comeback. I held my breath.

"Corinne, I know I'm leaving in a couple of weeks—three, to be exact—but I care for you and I want to do this. I want to see where this can go. Corinne, can we try? Can we try to be together?"

I stared into his eyes and realized he wasn't joking. He was the Owl of Minerva, spreading his wings at dusk and maybe realizing too late what we could have been.

This could be real—us. But could we rescue a future together before it slipped from our grasp? I was determined to form words despite the jumbled thoughts affecting my judgment. A knock at the door interrupted me.

"Corinne, we have to go! The cab's here." It was Donut. I looked at Curtis.

"I need to think about this." I got up and left, dragging my heart behind me in protest. I didn't know what to do. I ran out of the front door, saying quick good-byes, and dashed into the cab with my friend. That's what I'd been there to do: say good-bye.

I was supposed to be furious with Curtis. My mind said so. But my heart was no longer listening; it was careening, madly in love with a guy who was leaving in three weeks.

Escape

After we became an item, Curtis sent me a video he'd made of himself not long after I had left the party. Shirt off, in bed, and staring at the computer's webcam, he cursed the invisible me, recounting how we came to know each other and lamenting that his study-abroad experience was not supposed to include returning home with a long-distance girlfriend. He deliberated with himself, hashing out the pros and cons of committing to a relationship. He talked about future possibilities—ideas way ahead of my imaginings. He attempted to dissuade himself from asking me out, paused, then looked into the camera's lens, and decided to go for it. I'd never known his struggle, that he'd cared for me that much. His vulnerability and openness made me think this relationship could be something more than temporary.

However long we had—weeks, possibly continuing into summer, and then who knew?—the risk of being together, even for a little while, would be worth it. I wanted to step out and allow myself the indulgence of loving and being loved.

We held hands at school. I held my head high and stood tall. We sat together at the lunch table. During those final two weeks of school I walked around in a bubble, unaffected by the rest of the world. I couldn't wait to get to class where the teachers' lectures seemed livelier. I walked the halls and noticed the senior banners, the announcements decorating the walls—much more appealing than the drab tile floors I used to stare at. At night, we'd talk for hours on the phone or by Skype.

The two worlds I lived in played tug of war with my emotions. At one end, Curtis secured me and grounded me. On the other, my brother held me in a hangman's noose. My mother stood on the sidelines, acting like a judge without authority.

At home, she'd hear my brother's comments. They were out of line and hurtful. And yet she'd look at me, lower her voice, and tell me not to respond, to walk away. Where was the justice in that? Why was Corbin able to get away with treating his sister like that? But then again, what could my mother do?

One time she did go after him for his behavior. Corbin replied by yelling that she sucked as a mother. He then slammed his bedroom door. I watched as Mom paced quietly back and forth in the living room.

I guessed her concern centered on whether Corbin was in his room, cutting.

My mother compensated for her lack of power with skilled planning. She came into my room one night to deliver some news, snuggling up behind me and pulling me close. The pieces of us locked easily into place. Cuddling before bed had always been my favorite part of the day. I could hear Samson purring, perched above my head.

My mother had her faults. She made decisions I didn't agree with. But one thing was certain. We were close. I told my mother everything—about school, friends, boys, life. She'd listen and then ask a question or two. Sometimes my mother would give advice. She spoke of my strength and said that I had the gifts of wisdom and intuition and that those qualities would get me through life's challenges. I usually accepted her encouragement, but the problems with my brother made me think I might not be as strong as she thought.

That night, as we cuddled, my mother admitted she didn't know what to do about Corbin. She knew, however, what to do with me. Mom had arranged for the two of us to fly out the day after school ended. She wanted to separate my brother and me as soon as possible. She hoped plans to go to Colorado would give me something to look forward to. Dad and Corbin would stay behind in Singapore, attend counseling, and get to the root of Corbin's anger.

Colorado? Something to look forward to? Curtis would be in Colorado!

* * *

I stand in a dark and secluded room, absolutely still, not knowing where I am. The private sanctum is slowly transformed, sporadic beams of light illuminating pasty walls and pearl-tile floors. Memories of Corbin and me playing at the park flash on the barren wall in front of me. We enjoy our young, carefree life back in Dallas. To my left, there is another flash. Mom and Dad are laughing and hugging as my brother and I spray our three dogs during a game of fetch in the backyard.

I jump back as flames spread and then vanish from the floor in the middle of the room, revealing a scorched picture of a more recent time. Slowly, deliberately, I kneel down to take a closer look at the image of a family blown off course. Mom and Dad look older—and sad. There are only three of us in the photo. I trace the outline of an invisible form next to mine—a feeble attempt to include my brother in the spot where he belonged, next to me. The image melts into a thick crimson liquid. I am left standing in the middle of it, exposed and vulnerable. I quickly step away, backing myself into a corner.

The small pool rises from its dormant state and mutates into a network of veins and arteries slithering toward me, spreading like a web across the floor, encircling my ankles. In the middle of the room glistens a paring knife—and gripping it, an ashen hand. Attached to the hand is the icy white image of my twin. I scream his name. No answer. No matter how many times I yell for help, no matter how many times I plead for him, his glassy eyes remain glued to the floor, his right hand repeatedly slicing his paper-thin flesh as his image fades away.

My eyes unbolted and alert, I gasped for air as I looked around in the darkness of the cabin. *Where am I?* My mother was next to me, fast asleep. I began telling myself things I knew to be true. *It was only a nightmare. I am on a plane with my mother going to Colorado. My brother is alive back in Singapore with my father.*

I'm okay. I'm okay. I'm okay.

I thought about the nightmares. They had steadily increased to three or four a week, but I hid them from my parents. Their overworked hearts didn't need my added suffering. Usually I could rock myself back to sleep, alone in my misery. I'd become quite the pro at self-soothing. I looked over at my mother. The edges of her lip turned slightly upward, giving her a more youthful appearance. Was she dreaming of happier times? I didn't wake her, wanting desperately for her to stay sheltered in subconscious delusion.

I calmed myself by thinking about the few months I'd have with her. I thought about the freedom to do whatever we wanted when we wanted and the laughter we'd experience. I also thought about the things I'd do without her. I'd see Curtis in a couple of days, and soon after that I'd meet up with friends at camp. The pleasing thoughts lulled me back to sleep.

The Alexanders lived in an upper-class neighborhood that spoke volumes about the disciplined lives of the residents. Lawns were well manicured, and dogs remained within invisible fences. Mr. and Mrs. Alexander met at an Ivy League school while pursuing master's degrees. They made their children's education a priority.

I wondered what Curtis' mom would think of me. I put up my guard, but as she opened the door I immediately recognized her facial features, which were much like his. The resemblance soothed me. I hugged her. Formalities over, I entered the home. To the left, a hollow medieval knight in full armor— history. To the right, the sitting room and a beautiful wood-carved piano—the arts.

Two beagles ran to greet me, tails wagging. Two girls followed—twins, completely opposite in looks and in personality. I was immediately drawn to them and missed my own twin, who was so different from me. Curtis came down the stairs by twos and threes, every step toward me erasing my remaining insecurity. He had my complete and undivided attention.

Studying me as though he hadn't seen me in months, my boyfriend picked me up and held me for a long time in front of everyone, unconcerned about the public display of affection.

He then took my hand and led me out to the backyard hammock where we rocked back and forth to the gentle swaying of the Colorado pines. I imagined that we were the only people on the planet and that nature was serenading us. Adam and Eve must have had a hammock in their garden; I pictured us there, in that first garden, destined to be together by divine decree.

I fell out of the webbed cot to avoid round two of a tickle fight, opting for a game of chase around the yard. Our mothers sat at the patio table, exchanging compliments and chatting about summer plans.

As the sun began to set, Curtis invited me to follow him through an opening in the trees that led to a park beyond a baseball diamond. Night came quickly lying in his arms on the soft grass, talking about nothing and everything.

"We should pick a star," I said.

He agreed. "Let's pick one inside a constellation so we always know where it is." His voice soothed me as I contemplated the impact of assigning a feeling to something I would see for the rest of my life.

"What's your favorite?" I wondered out loud.

"The Big Dipper … or Orion."

I noticed the Big Dipper right away. I wanted something we could pick out in any night sky, and the Dipper was on display all year in our part of the northern hemisphere. (I later learned that the ladle pattern itself isn't considered a constellation but consists of seven stars that belong to the larger Ursa Major, the celestial Big Bear—Oso in Spanish. This pattern circles the North Star every twenty-four hours, or about the time it takes for me to get to Curtis by plane.)

The Big Dipper, a perfect choice. Now for the star.

My focus shifted to the end of the handle. I traced the outline of the formation and settled on the deep end of the bowl section, gazing at the two Pointer stars that give the direction to the North Star, well known for helping people find their way. I always wanted to be able to find my way back to Curtis, but I was looking for something more subtle, more unique.

"I've got it. See the handle's end on the Big Dipper?" I asked.

"Yeah. I see it."

"Not that one. The one next to it, second one in."

"Is that our star?"

"That's ours. Only ours."

Curtis hugged me.

"Corinne, I want you to know that I love you more than all the stars in all the galaxies in all the universe. Remember that your knight will always be looking up at the heavens and thinking about you."

Affirmations from Curtis refueled my confidence. Now it was time to reunite with old friends at Young Life Camp. I looked forward to finding myself again and repairing hidden wounds.

The camp ran two weeks, from the third week of June through the first week of July. There I found a sheltered retreat where hardships couldn't reach me. Because Young Life served as an outreach ministry for God, I felt I'd found my chance to ask Him for help. If God was going to listen to me, it would be in a place like this.

I had a blast the first couple of days, making new friendships and rekindling old ones. I went swimming in the summer heat, played volleyball and soccer, and welcomed the camp competitions. For a brief moment I forgot about the sorrow of losing the relationship with my brother. I pretended I was another person in another life—happy through and through for the first time in a long while.

Counselors confiscated our phones in the mornings, but at night we could call our parents to check in. On the night of July 3, I picked up my phone to call my mom and discovered six missed calls, all from her.

I ran to a secluded room, fumbled for the callback button, and waited for her to answer.

When she picked up I sensed distress in her voice. As the conversation ended, I didn't know whether to smash my phone or to run away. I assumed the plan of separation and counseling came with a solution for our family. But no one and nothing could help us. Not some healing absence. Not the professionals. Not God.

I made my way back to our common room and sat on my bunk just as my friends returned from dinner. The six girls saw my tears and rushed in around me. It would take effort to recount our family troubles.

My mother had informed me of a change in plans. My brother was flying to the States and would land in Colorado the following day, July 4. Days before, early in the morning—and only hours ahead of a scheduled counseling appointment with my dad—Corbin had marched into a tattoo studio in Far East Plaza on Scotts Road and had emerged branded across his back and shoulder blades with "People = Shit" in large letters.

Corbin had been warned. Time and time again, he'd asked about getting a tattoo. Dad remained adamant when it came to tattoos and piercings. The answer was no. He assured Corbin the consequences of defying him would not be enjoyable. I guess Corbin, after pushing the limits, thought Dad might ground him, yell at him, or take his phone. It must have caught my brother by surprise when Dad called the airlines immediately after finding out about the tattoo and told Corbin to pack his bags—for good.

Dad viewed the tattoo as a cry for help, particularly given what it said. The tattoo also confirmed that Dad had lost control of the situation. So had Corbin, given the drinking, the cutting, the missed curfews, the depression, and the increased illicit behavior. Dad had hoped love and counseling could change Corbin's direction. However, the early morning tattoo received moments before a counseling appointment made quite a statement. My brother was obstinate in his defiance. Dad decided Corbin needed a radical change in environment. My part in the drama, however, proved more difficult to define.

Mom said I could stay at camp or go to my uncle's house in Castle Rock where she would stay with Corbin for a couple of days. Corbin had a good relationship with Uncle Carter. My uncle—calm, practical, without judgment—could buffer the strain between my brother and my disappointed and worried mom. She said Corbin wouldn't be there long. I asked her when I would see him again if I decided to remain at camp. Mom said she didn't know.

The following day my mother drove two hours to pick me up. As she cradled me in her arms, my world fell out beneath me. Both of us sobbed quietly in unison. We didn't have to say it: our peaceful summer had come to an abrupt and devastating end.

Even though my brother's presence frightened me, I was still happy to see him. I ran through the entryway of my uncle's house to greet him, but Corbin huffed and pushed me aside as if shooing away a mangy stray begging for scraps. Feeling worthless and unwanted, I retreated to the guest room bed and propped up my body with pillows and pity.

The next morning I tiptoed around my uncle's house as if it were filled with shattered glass. One wrong move could provoke a painful situation. Not surprisingly, my brother stayed in his own world, barely speaking to anyone or showing emotion. The only laughter I heard from my brother came later in the day when he and Uncle Carter talked about sports.

Other sounds I remember came from phone calls between my mother and father talking about Corbin. The options were military school or a camp for at-risk teenagers. After the calls, Mom would pace in reflection until some insight directed her to the computer for more research. She'd try to talk to Corbin, but more often than not her attempts escalated into shouting matches. I'd escape to the bathroom and shut the door. The handle on the sink provided the only relief I could find. I'd turn the water on full force and watch as my tears joined the rushing water, drowning the evidence of my weeping. I'd empty myself of feeling and then stare in the mirror. I realized there that I had no control over my life—or anyone or anything. Whenever I escaped to the bathroom to practice my drowning technique, one thought captured me: something could be waiting for me around the corner and up the stairs, something even worse than what came before. That constant thought—of something worse around the corner—haunted me.

After two more eternal days with my brother, my father joined us from Singapore. He seemed older. I couldn't blame the grueling twenty-four-hour flight. Not this time. His thinning hairline, bloodshot eyes, pale skin, and defeated countenance were signs of stress taking its toll. I'd never seen Daddy so frail. I'd always known him as strong, independent, and competitive. This man ran marathons, climbed Mount Kilimanjaro, explored rural India, lifted in the gym five times a week, and thrived on the adrenaline rush of adventure. He'd been the most capable man I'd ever known, but now he appeared broken and feeble. Anger and concern welled up inside me. As I embraced him, he squeezed me tight. I didn't want to let him go, but he pulled back from me.

"Corinne, have you lost weight?" he asked.

I had—approximately five pounds since he'd last seen me a month earlier. I wasn't trying to lose weight. I just wasn't hungry. Dad narrowed his eyes and smiled. I enjoyed his protective nature.

As I watched him take hold of my mother, I saw my brother's eyes roll in disgust. My mother's body relaxed. Her hand gestures changed. I took note of the graceful way she embraced my father's neck. My mother appeared so sure of herself as she smiled at him, but I knew better. (The growing array of over-the-counter remedies for stomach ailments next to her makeup bag gave her away.)

The day after Dad arrived, he and Corbin left for our grandparents' home in Vail where they'd pick up Grandpa and head for Idaho to drop my brother off at the School of Urban and Wilderness Survival (SUWS), that camp for at-risk teenagers. Dad concluded there'd be less chance of an argument if he brought along Grandpa—someone Corbin respected. I don't think Dad had any idea how long Corbin would stay at the camp. How could he know what awaited my brother in the desert? But the highly recommended program had a proven track record of helping teens in distress, and that certainly defined my brother.

My mother and I remained in Castle Rock with my uncle and his family. In a few days, we'd head up to Vail where we'd regroup with Dad and talk about … what? The life we had no control over? Plan B for the summer?

When it was time to leave, Mom and I drove up I-70 on the way to my grandparent's house, giving me a couple of hours to reflect. My mind drifted to Bible stories of long ago. I wanted something to grab hold of, something I could relate to. I settled on three young men—Shadrach, Meshach, and Abednego—thrown into a fiery furnace because of their faith. I had faith. I believed in God. And I also understood that tests and trials would come to those who believed. But I noticed a marked difference between them and me.

The three faithful Jews had walked through the fire unbound and unharmed. Not so for me. I ran around my furnace panicked over the scorching, the pain, and the heat. What did this mean? Was I missing something? Did I not have enough faith? Maybe I wasn't measuring up, even with God. Where was He anyway?

I thought maybe He still lived back in the Old Testament days, preferring to show Himself to the present generations through His miracles back then. He existed beyond the realm of time, right? Maybe He favored hanging out with the great saints of the older books—Abraham, Moses, David. My thoughts returned to my predicament. The book of Daniel revealed a fourth character in that fire—some say the form appeared like the Son of God. I had to admit that I'd also found help in the midst of the flames that engulfed me, but it wasn't God who had come to my rescue, not directly anyway.

I found my life swinging like a pendulum between the maddening events unfolding within my family and the giddiness I felt with my boyfriend. Newton's law of motion was playing itself out: after every intense moment of pain came an equal and opposite moment of absolute pleasure.

Curtis' upcoming birthday stirred my creativity. I couldn't believe his parents agreed he could spend such an important milestone with me. I wasn't about to let his big day pass without doing my best to make him feel special.

I wanted to arrange every detail. Mom and I weighed the dinner options then drove to a restaurant in Lionshead Village. Looking at the menu, she hovered over the steak options while I searched the side dishes.

"Do you see something he'll like?"

"Yes, definitely." Chophouse Mac n' Big Cheese. He couldn't resist good old mac and cheese. We reserved a table for two outside with a view of the gondola and the mountain behind it.

Mom and I selected a carrot cake at a nearby bakery and topped it with the number sixteen. We cleaned Grandma's greenhouse, modeled after I.M. Pei's glass pyramid at the Louvre. I tested the dimmer switch for the stringed lights around the plants. As we worked, I played Curtis' birthday over and over through my mind: an early birthday dinner, a ride up the gondola to watch the sunset, then ending the celebration at the greenhouse with cake and lights and memories. It had to be perfect. Every detail. Mom and I finished the prep work then drove to Denver the following morning to retrieve the one I'd worked so hard to please.

On the way back, my anticipation increased as the car turned off the paved two-lane road and onto a gravel path then through the valley of a neighbor's open range. The car slowed to a crawl. Curious Highland cattle blocked the route. I never minded their congregating in the middle of the road, but the idea of making our way through the herd always made me a little uneasy.

We knew from experience that no amount of honking or yelling would redirect these stubborn creatures. A gentle forward march with an exposed front bumper was the only answer. Lucky for us, these Scottish breeds with long horns and wavy coats submitted to the prodding and gave way, though only after several attempts. I bet if it came down to a duel, the Highlands would come out on top.

We passed the roadblock and continued our journey up the switchbacks. I couldn't place the queasiness in my stomach. Was it the back-and-forth motion of the mountain terrain or my unease about bringing the first guy I ever cared about to the land where I found serenity?

"I'm looking forward to seeing your cabin," Curtis said.

In the rearview mirror I could see a slight grin emerge on my mother's face. Pulling up to the custom-made iron gate, she rolled down the driver's seat window and entered a four-digit code on the control panel recessed within a stone column. The gate buzzed and opened, granting access to the place I called home.

The aspen-lined drive curved past a bolted wooden trash shed donned with claw marks up one side—failed bear attempts at beef bourguignon drippings. We turned on to the stone driveway. Mom instinctively raised her arm slightly and pressed the garage-door button on the visor. A copper-plated panel slowly rose, revealing the contents of the garage: a hunter-green 911 Carrera convertible, a silver 911 Targa, a night-blue Audi A8, and a black 1934 Ford with a license plate that spelled "COOOL." Grandpa would soon trade in the green 911 for a black-and-silver R8, but to me it was just another combination of letters and numbers. Curtis didn't say a word. Somehow I knew he wouldn't.

"There's something I want to show you," I said.

Mom walked toward a door on the left that led to the stairway, while Curtis grabbed his overnight bag and followed me around a wall on the right. We reached a solid oak door that led to an elevator. Once Curtis and I entered the lift, I first had to close the door then slide an accordion partition into the locked position before the elevator could engage.

I depressed the second-floor button, which obediently lit. The elevator jerked upward. Curtis dropped his bag and thrust me against the wall. His mouth and his smell engulfed me. I reached over, found the elevator's protruding red stop knob, and pressed it.

The elevator, now immobile between two floors, wrapped us in privacy. Neither upstairs nor downstairs doors could be opened until the lift reached its destination. We would take what we could get, seeing as my parents didn't favor dramatic displays of public affection.

I wondered if adults ever had moments like these. Did my parents or grandparents ever steal away in this elevator and purposely press the stop button? On one hand, I hoped not. I wanted more of Curtis in this moment without those thoughts running through my head. On the other hand, I never wanted to be too old to feel this spontaneous or this passionate.

My body tingled and shivered in response to his gentle kisses. I pulled the stop button, activating the elevator once again. I couldn't risk a lecture at the beginning of his two-day stay. Curtis followed me to the guest bedroom with a helpless look on his face. He dropped his overnight gear on the floor next to one of two twin-sized beds. He would have the room to himself. Mom and Dad said I could stay in the other guest room, along with them—Dad would confine himself to the far edge of the king-sized bed while Mom would spoon me on the side facing the door.

The tour of the guest quarters was brief, mainly focusing on the views. The point of my mission was out back. Steering Curtis back down the hall, we retraced our steps past the elevator and toward the side door of the main kitchen. Stepping outside, our eyes were drawn to the magnificence of the snow-capped Gore Range glistening off in the distance. The view was breathtaking.

Grandpa's ranch rested atop thirty acres of prime real estate outside of Vail. In this wildlife sanctuary, big game seemed to know the exact date when hunters would be let loose on the adjacent public land. Elk and deer would congregate on Grandpa's property the day before shots rang throughout the valley. It was July, not hunting season yet, but small herds would still sometimes make an appearance at dusk around the ridge of his land.

I led Curtis down a stone path lined with lupine and coreopsis. A flowing stream on the right ended at a pond stocked with fish. To the left, a hammock beckoned us to softly swing in the gentle breeze. Hammocks—something else we had in common. The first time I'd visited his house, we'd reclined on his backyard hammock and swayed under the pines.

And now we were rocking back and forth, feeding each other Mike and Ike Original Fruit candies and whispering sweet nothings in each other's ears. Amid the gentle rustling of the aspen leaves, we slowly drifted to sleep, resting in the mid-afternoon sun before celebrating the night that turned out just as I'd hoped.

Our path down to the hammock by the pond.

Trust Is a Traitor

Having my father around brought calm back into my life. I often call him my Atticus Finch. A character résumé titled "Bridge Builder" rests on my father's desk alongside a row of family pictures. His degrees and certificates of stature remain rolled up in a tube in a corner of his office, collecting dust. He prefers peacemaking and patient endurance in the midst of trials, his reassuring voice calmly exploring opportunities during the most trying times. When he was around I followed him everywhere he went, seeking his comfort and protection.

Near the end of the summer, Dad asked me to dinner. When I was a young girl, I'd called these our daddy-daughter dates. Our nights together evoked grand ideas of a king and a princess attending the symphony or dining in a fine restaurant—or feeding the ducks. Those nights were set aside just for us, and Daddy would remind me of my importance.

The summer day grew dim; time to get dressed. The crisp Colorado air chilled my skin, so I chose a long, cream-colored sweater with black tights and slick leather boots. I walked down the long hallway into the living room. My father sat patiently reading a book on my grandparents' couch. He'd heard my steps on the wooden floor and looked up. He smiled. His approving eyes warmed my heart. Every time my father saw me on our date nights it was as if he were looking at me for the first time.

"There's my princess!" He stood and gave me a hug. "You look beautiful." I laughed.

"Dad, you always say that." My father looked down at me and kissed the top of my head.

"Only because it's true. I never want you to forget how beautiful you are, so I'm going to keep on reminding you. You okay with that?"

I nodded. It felt good to smile with my father after the hardships we'd encountered that year. We walked arm in arm down the stairs into the garage. My father ran ahead of me to open the passenger door of the Audi. He was skilled at making me feel special.

As we drove, I suddenly became disoriented. We had turned right toward Cordillera instead of left toward town.

"Dad, where are we going?" My father's eyes focused on the road.

"Oh, you'll see."

I laughed. My father loved surprising me. We soon turned left and approached a tall, elegant black gate protected by two security guards.

"Dad … You didn't."

He smiled at me. "Oh yes, I did."

My father waved to the security guard, who motioned us through.

We drove up a windy road and pulled into a parking lot where we got out of the car and walked up some stone steps and into a lodge. I followed my father into the restaurant where a waiter pulled out my chair, placed a napkin in my lap, and handed me a menu with the word *Mirador* on the cover. It had been years since we'd come up here. Mom and Dad had spent their honeymoon in this hotel. Corbin and I had taken golf lessons out on the greens. We'd lunched outside at Grouse on the Green while overlooking the Vail Valley. I paused and absorbed the candlelit setting.

"Corinne, this is a special night, so I want you to pick anything you want off of the menu, okay?"

I hadn't been eating a lot with all the stress, but that night I resolved to enjoy myself. My father and I laughed as we swapped stories about my attempts to drive a golf cart and about how butterflies or roly polies would distract me from finding my ball in the rough, luring me off course and irritating the party of four behind us.

We ate our fill; Dad enjoyed the beef tenderloin and roasted potatoes while I savored the beet salad and grilled salmon. We even ordered dessert, deciding to split one. Our stomachs were full, but we couldn't pass on chocolate lava cake. The two of us grinned when the waiter placed before us the steaming dessert topped with a scoop of the chef's homemade ice cream. I grabbed my spoon, ready to pounce, as my father began to speak.

"Corinne, I can't tell you how much I've treasured this night with you."

"I love you too, Daddy," I said, hypnotized by the fudge oozing out of the chocolate mold. My spoon began to tease more goo from its hiding place.

"It's about your mother," he said.

I realized he'd been talking for a while, but I'd missed something.

"What's wrong, Dad? Is she okay?"

His expression turned solemn. He'd been hiding something from me.

"Dad, what is it?" I asked as I put down my spoon, waiting for a reply.

"Corinne." My father addressed me in a way that made me uneasy, his soft tone and serious gaze alerting me that the mood of the night was about to change. I sat up straight, bracing for this uninvited encroachment into what had been a night of warm recollections.

He continued, "Corinne, your brother won't be coming home."

I sank into my chair, not wanting to draw attention in a public place.

"After his camp is over, your mother and I have decided to send Corbin to boarding school. It's in Maine."

I didn't know how to respond. Yes, I had been upset and even mad at my brother, but I thought camp would fix everything and he'd come home. Dad searched my eyes for feedback. I didn't give much, so he continued.

"The advice we're getting is that he shouldn't be placed back in the same environment he came from. Apparently there's an 80 percent failure rate if he comes back home right after camp."

I was shocked and angry at Corbin and at my parents, and I'm sure my eyes conveyed that message.

"So why did you say, 'It's about your mother?' What does this have to do with Mom?"

"Petunia, we can't abandon him."

My heart skipped a beat. What did that mean? My shock and anger turned into apprehension. What was he not saying?

"Dad, I know all this," I responded, my stern voice taking over. "What's going on?" My father sat up straight and took my hands. His grip was firm but gentle.

"Corinne, your mother's not coming back with us either." I jerked my hands away from his.

"What? What are you saying to me? Dad!" He might as well have slapped me.

"Your mother and I have talked about it. She needs to be in the States to make sure Corbin knows we still care."

I dropped my head and focused on the napkin in my lap. I wanted to scream in front of everyone. Why was I being punished? Why was my mother leaving me? What about me? What about caring for me? Did anyone see me? Did my father see me? He pressed on.

"If we're all over in Singapore as one happy family without him, it could be devastating for him—for all of us."

I agreed with that part. What he'd said about being separated would most certainly be devastating.

"Corinne, you'll be all right. Okay? You'll be with me."

I picked up the silver spoon and drew chocolate swirls in the vanilla froth that had been my ice cream. For a moment there was only silence. Our night of pure bliss had been engulfed by nauseating dead air.

"Corinne, I'm so sorry. I didn't want …"

I glared at him.

"Stop. Just … stop. It's fine. I'm fine."

I wasn't fine. I was angry and hurt, but I wasn't about to let him see that.

"Can we please go?"

His eyes probed my face, trying to read my emotions. Ever so gently, he replied, "Sure, Petunia. Let's go home."

I went mute. Numbed by pain and wounded feelings, I fell completely silent. There was nothing I could say, nothing I wanted to say. I had no vote. No voice. No opinion that mattered.

The next few days went by without much conversation. I answered questions with as few words as possible, consumed by my own thoughts. *How could Mom leave me? How could she abandon her own daughter after everything I've done, everything I've tried to do? Even though I've suffered by striving to stay strong for my family, I'm going to be left behind. Why am I being punished for something I didn't do?*

With all of these unanswered questions, I became bitter. Innocent-but-strong Corinne disappeared while a new shell of a Corinne emerged. Brick by brick, a wall of protection rose against outsiders and family alike. It would soon be so high and so thick that I'd begin to cut people out of my life one by one, knowing if I didn't make the move first, sooner or later others would make that move on me. I had to shed myself of this traitorous notion called trust.

It's hard for me to look back and relive the emotions of that time. I returned to my pseudo-home near the equator. My brother continued to struggle with his personal battles. I didn't realize or understand the tremendous amount of pain he'd internalized and endured. I also found out one of the reasons my mother had remained in the States—she'd developed a chronic illness and sought help at the Cooper Clinic in Dallas.

My parents hadn't divulged just how sick she'd been. She had stomach-lining bleeding or something similar (apparently stress-related). They didn't want to worry me, but not telling me made my head spin. I obsessed over the reasons she remained in the States, leaving me on my own. I loved my dad, but he traveled. His business trips lasted a few days and took place here and there. He said that I'd be okay, that our helper would look after me. But she wasn't Mom. I needed my mother.

I found no way to cope. My brother had betrayed me. My mother—abandoned me. I wanted to disappear, but how? I couldn't kill myself. I didn't want to cause anyone pain, and I knew if I hurt myself, my parents would be devastated. I wasn't one to experiment. I couldn't even stand the smell of smoke. Where was my answer then? Where was my escape?

There's a saying that we aren't given more than we can handle. Who said that? I believe the opposite is true. My brother had been given more than he could handle. So had I. People are often given more than they can handle. Some come through the fire. Some don't. I wouldn't have come out had it not been for Curtis, who repeatedly reached into that furnace to offer me relief.

The Corset

November 2009, junior year. The flu was raging through Southeast Asia and in my body. Feverish hallucinations took me to scenes of destruction and loss I didn't wish to revisit—places and people I'd seen over the last seven years while traveling Asia: a drugged and drooling rented-out baby draped over the arm of a young girl who had forced her free hand into our tour van to ask for money; sun-bear hides for sale by those who were supposed to protect them; tiger parts made into necklaces; monkey carcasses lying on the road near rows of planted palm trees; coral reefs killed off by fishermen using dynamite.

I'd wake up shivering and panicked about my thoughts, yearning for my mother's reassuring cuddles. I'd tell myself it had to be the fever, and then I'd drift back into the same dreadful visions. I missed a week of classes, not good for someone who struggled with the academic rigor of the Singapore American School. I also lost weight—and the chance to play rugby. I told

WHERE THE MONSTER WEIGHTS

myself missing tryouts was probably for the best. I was tired and emotionally drained, and my reserves would have to be spent on makeup work anyway.

Had it been only ten days since October break? Ten days since I'd seen Curtis? Happy memories distracted me from negativity—my seventeenth birthday gift, a trip home to see Mom and visit Curtis.

When I felt better I relapsed into worry over the academic goliath taunting me. I didn't even know where to begin with all the schoolwork I had to do. I sucked at math and had a makeup exam to study for. Honor roll? Out of the question this semester. I was too far behind. I called my mother to confess my anxiety. She recounted past times I had struggled and persevered. She reminded me of my discipline and determination. She listed the positives in my life. I agreed. What did I have to complain about? Blessings surrounded me. I had an amazing boyfriend. I traveled. I wasn't starving. I had a roof over my head.

As I hung up the phone, however, my thoughts returned to rugby and to school—this time to the social aspects. My identity hung in the balance. I no longer belonged to a team. Puppy Love e-mails filled my inbox. Could I continue to manage the club and handle my academics?

On the first morning back at school, I walked through the gate and quickly ran into people I knew. Many of them commented on my looks. They asked if I'd lost weight. I thought I looked the same. My uniform skirt fit lower on my hips than I remembered, but it wasn't low enough to cause this kind of attention. Maybe they'd missed me.

Bounding up the steps, I passed a popular girl who said hello. We'd walked by each other many times before and she'd never noticed me, much less offered a greeting. I had to admit I enjoyed the recognition. I approached the school office doors and pulled out my doctor's note.

"Hi, Corinne!"

I looked up to see one of my mother's friends. Adults, especially Mom's friends, were going out of their way to talk to me now that my mother and brother were gone. I'd fill them in on my brother, saying he enjoyed the cold weather in Maine, played football for his boarding school, and that his new favorite snack was something called a Whoopie Pie. Mom was still visiting family, and yes, I missed them very much. Mom's friends seemed concerned about me and even gave me gifts. Their well-meaning efforts, however, only reminded me of my family's absence. I prepared myself for the usual questions as her friend approached.

"You look great! Have you lost weight?" she asked.

Well, that was unexpected. I said I had and that I'd been sick but was feeling better now. I thanked her for the compliment and told her I had to get to class, but as I walked away, I noticed something inside me changing. The last pieces of a puzzle were forming into a picture I hadn't seen before—an answer to the void.

I turned in my medical slip and went to class. I watched the teacher's lips move, but I wasn't listening. I was busy processing something else. People had noticed me. Not for my grades. Not for sports. They didn't ask about Puppy Love. They'd affirmed that I'd achieved something else, something of value. I'd been sick, very sick, and I'd lost weight. And people praised me for it.

I'd lost so much lately—much more than weight. The stress of thinking about the loss of rugby and the catch-up work overwhelmed me. *Get your head back in the game, Corinne. You can't afford to fall behind more than you already have.* I shook my head and tuned back in to the class discussion, but the processing continued running in the background.

That day I walked into the cafeteria and was confronted by the aroma of Mr. Hoe's fried rice and sesame chicken, my favorite. My stomach rumbled. But as I made my way toward the hot-meal line, I balked. To my right, a smaller station with fewer people captured my attention—the salad bar.

I scanned the options: chicken, ham, chickpeas, cheese, croutons, veggies. As I considered my choices, Mr. Hoe's chicken called out to me. What did I want to do—satisfy a desire for what I wanted at the moment or show myself there was still something in my life I could manage, something I could control? I had to succeed at something—anything. One small exercise in self-control might make me feel better. *Done. Salad it is.* I'd be in charge of what went into my salad and how much I wanted. I counted this as a win. It felt good not only to win, but to eat right. I determined right there and then to make "healthy" choices a priority.

After school, I went home and said hello to Rosie, our helper. I glanced over her shoulder, curious about dinner. She smiled and continued to busy herself by cutting up veggies for a shrimp stir-fry. I grabbed a bowl of grapes from the fridge and sat on the couch with my computer. I typed in the words *shrimp stir-fry* and *calories.* Not bad. I called out to Rosie and asked her to use only a teaspoon of oil. I searched more websites about foods, especially foods for weight loss. Maybe I could be good at this. I researched the calorie counts of foods I usually ate when I came home from school: queso and chips, cereal with milk, nachos, veggies with ranch dressing. I couldn't believe I'd gotten away with eating like that. How could I still have looked athletic? I realized I probably burned a lot of calories from practice and games. But I didn't play rugby anymore. No more rugby, no more queso.

I wondered what foods were considered healthy. After a while, I heard Rosie setting the table.

"Corinne … dinner."

I looked at the time and then back at the long document I'd prepared listing foods and their calorie count.

Rosie had piled my plate with shrimp stir-fry and brown rice. Rice was a carb. The body uses carbs for energy. I didn't need energy at night. If a carb wasn't used for energy, it might be stored … as fat. *Eww.* I took the plate into the kitchen, grabbed a spoon, scooped the stir-fry off of the rice, and put the mixture on a clean plate. Leaving the rice behind, I stepped over to the pan and added more shrimp to my dish.

I thanked Rosie for the meal and asked her to please get Vitamin Water Zero from the store—a lot of it. Any flavor would do. I also asked for jicama, a low-calorie root vegetable that looked like a turnip and tasted like a sweet water chestnut. I could snack on that in the afternoons and count it as a carb if necessary. Success! My first day as the new me.

Lunches became limited to the salad bar. After each visit, I'd research the ingredients I ate, adjust, and plan for an even healthier option next time. Restricting became a secret game I played with myself. Croutons were the first to go. I loved their crunch and flavor, but research revealed they were an unnecessary carb.

Out they went. Dressing followed. I had never before measured how much ranch I poured over my salad. I thought the creamy texture made the salad complete, but after further research, whenever I looked at my favorite dressing, I saw fat. I decided to forgo the ranch and eat my salad dry. It wasn't that bad. I started to appreciate the taste of the fresh veggies. I still added a scoop of cheese and some chicken on top.

One month later I ditched the chicken. Cheese provided both calcium and protein, so I didn't need chicken. Choosing smaller bowls for my salad selection, I didn't have to worry about consumption. I could eat everything in my bowl and still participate in the conversations around me. At the end of each meal, I would mentally acknowledge my accomplishment of eating less than everyone else. When my friends would comment about my eating habits and about how gross it must be to eat salad without dressing, I'd respond by defending the natural taste of fresh ingredients, redirecting their increasing observations into some harmless absurdity of mine.

What had started as a goal to lose a little more weight became something more. The holiday season meant fudge for teachers and cookies for neighbors. One day Rosie and I busied ourselves in the kitchen baking sugar cookies. The smell tempted me. I reached for a warm and freshly iced sample and took a big bite without thought. Around the fourth chew,

I impulsively bent over a plastic garbage bag hanging on the kitchen door and emptied all the contents of my mouth. Rosie had her back to me as she iced more cookies. I returned to her side, saying, "Yum!"

I obsessed over my eating. I began making up rules and boundaries and rewards. I bargained with myself. If I was hungry after lunch, I'd drink water to fill me. Bored with water, I chewed gum. That would distract me enough until I got home, where hunger pangs hit the hardest. That's when the reward came into play. If I made it through that pain until it subsided, I could eat a whole jicama. Rosie would have it peeled and sliced and waiting in the fridge.

I decided home was where I'd welcome the pain head on as some sort of self-mutilation. There, I could concentrate on it and dissect it. I even researched it. I read that hunger pangs don't actually indicate hunger and, in fact, are a cause of overeating due to the response to these false feelings. Hunger pangs actually come from the stomach lining rubbing against itself merely because the stomach is empty and at rest. Apparently stomachs need rest too.

I convinced myself that every cramp, every pain could be a false sensation, same as hunger pangs. What other feelings could be misinterpreted? Could other things I thought were true actually be false? The pain from restricting my food intake provided an acceptable substitute for the emotional loss, which I preferred not to examine. At least I could control the source of my hunger pangs. I could choose whether to feed my body and to alleviate the ache. So the pain was something I looked forward to—a kind of pleasure to anticipate and then toy with. But the semester's end approached, and that meant reuniting with family around favorite meals. It couldn't be a bad thing to eat at one of my favorite restaurants, could it?

Daddy and I flew to the States for the holidays where we met up with Mom and Corbin in Colorado. I screamed their names when I saw them. Mom looked healthy. Corbin gave me a big hug. We all piled in the car and headed up I-70 toward Vail. And sure enough, on the way, we stopped for dinner at Beau Jo's to celebrate.

I must have been caught up in the emotion of it all: the four of us together, talking and laughing like we used to do. The thick-crust cheese and pepperoni pizza arrived at our table. I ate with my family. Corbin and I exchanged school stories. Corbin said he couldn't wait to hit the slopes. I grabbed the honey from the middle of the table and drizzled it over the remaining portion of crust on my plate. My brother looked good—and happy to be with us. My heart warmed as he smiled at me. The bill came and I took one last bite of crust before getting up from the table.

Conversation continued as Dad drove the rental car up to my grandparents' house where I said a quick hello to my grandparents and made my way to the guest room. Mom tucked me in and told me how much she loved me. When she left, I closed my eyes and thought it couldn't have been a better day.

Then, out of nowhere, came a tight knot in my gut. I sat straight up in bed, grabbed my stomach, and bent over. *What is wrong with me?* I shook my head and remembered. The pizza. I shivered as I tried to recall how many pieces I'd eaten—two, maybe three. I sat for a bit until the blockage moved somewhere less offensive. Then I threw back the covers and tiptoed toward the guest-room door. I had to be quiet. My parents slept in the bedroom next to mine. I could hear muffled sounds coming from the living-room TV. I found my brother lying on the couch.

"Corinney, come sit next to me," he said softly.

"Hey, Corby," I said. "Let me check something on the computer first, okay?"

I had to know. How many calories? How much fat? What was the damage? I walked past my brother and took a seat at the kitchen counter next to Dad's laptop. I clicked "Guest" on his computer screen and typed in a word search for the restaurant's nutritional page. The pizza was broken down into categories of crust, sauce, toppings, and cheeses. I added up the calories, fats, and carbs for three pieces. *My addition must be wrong. I'm bad at math, and it's late.* I added again. And again. I checked the numbers on the nutrition page to confirm what I'd written down. *Too much. Way too much.* I stared at the keyboard while rubbing my temples with the tips of my fingers.

Corinne, how could you let that slip? You knew you might go there. It's your favorite restaurant in Denver. Why didn't you look up the fat and calories before you went? You lost control. How could you not be aware of what you were eating? You let people distract you. If you can't mange what you eat, maybe you shouldn't eat at all. At least not in a risky situation. Not where you can be distracted!

I hugged Corbin and told him we could hang out in the morning. I promised we'd bundle up and go out in the snow. I went to my room and closed the door. *Sit-ups. Do sit-ups until you can't do them anymore.* I got down on the floor and didn't make a sound, going up and down until I could no longer lift my head. I swore to myself I'd be more careful next time.

And I was. Christmas was only days away. The holiday meant feasting and that scared me, so I welcomed the increased personal health awareness and advice. Except this advice, this third-person voice in my head giving instruction, had begun to surface unexpectedly and sometimes uninvited. My suspicions about this intruder were confirmed on the morning of Christmas Eve when Grandpa brought out the raclette grill. I waited next to him as he assembled the contraption and then hugged him in appreciation for family traditions. I pictured melted cheese dripping over ham, pickles, pearl onions, and red potatoes. I thought about how Grandpa would stand over the grill that evening and serve us all with joy on his face.

Then the inner voice reminded me of the vow I had made to myself not to be caught up in distraction. It told me to leave the kitchen. I obeyed. I left the tempting smells of simmering sauces on the stove to examine gifts under the tree. I breathed in the pine scent and thought of my family nearby. The voice approved.

At dinner, I accepted the raclette with a smile. I sat at the table and commented on the delicious food before me. But as I sat, the voice coached me on the art of distraction. It taught me to gesture animatedly with my hands and to speak loudly when people looked at me. That way they were less likely to notice the contents on my plate. I thought the advice was getting a little out of hand, but I didn't know what to do about it. Could I tell my mother? What would I say? I didn't know how to make sense of what was happening to me. Was I supposed to tell her someone or something was talking to me inside my head? That sounded crazy. And I didn't think I was crazy.

During that winter break, I researched more foods and more restaurants. I lost more weight and received more compliments about my looks, even from Mom. I obsessed over all kinds of food—what was in it, how to avoid it, how much I wanted it. I also thought about how much I weighed. I'd sneak into my grandmother's closet where she kept her scale. I would weigh myself a couple of times a day. At the end of each day, I'd double-check everything I ate to make sure I remained under my set daily limit for calories and fat.

Short reprieves came during visits with Curtis. We spent time together and with his friends, a tight-knit group I found easy to be around. One of his friends in particular was becoming a close friend of mine.

I met Zazzy Brown only once during the previous summer, but the connection was immediate. Her personality matched her name. Spunky and full of whit, she kept my mind at work just trying to keep up with her. During that autumn we got to know each other—posting video messages several times a week on each other's Facebook walls and chatting on Skype, sometimes during my free periods at school. I admired her. She managed a job, All-State choir, and high academic performance with ease. My October visit to see Curtis included some time with Zazzy, but by winter, our friendship had grown into an identity apart from Curtis. I invited her up to the house in Vail for some girl time.

We walked around Vail Village, ice skated at Beaver Creek, and attended a groundbreaking ceremony for a residential summer camp, partially founded by my grandparents. We drank hot cider, wrote messages of wellness on the pre-cut timber for the camp, and focused on catching up during the limited time we had together.

Even so, I took note of the increased attention from both guys—whistling—and women—asking if I had a portfolio, wanting to know if I modeled. The corruption in my head was swelling, recording every detail, and becoming more aware of the inverse relationship between weight and compliments. I wondered if I should decrease my daily calories to see if I could improve the speed of my weight loss. But each time I considered the seduction of the world and compliments and weight loss, something about my boyfriend caused an irritating jab to the voice and its truthfulness.

Each day, my boyfriend used some form of communication to describe the beauty he saw in me. In fact, I recalled that he'd told me how beautiful I was when I weighed 117. Back when I played rugby. Before I got the flu and lost weight. Before the voice came. Before I weighed 104. That didn't make sense.

Something else didn't make sense. The number on the scale decreased but the size of my stomach increased. How could that be? I thought I must have been chewing too much gum. Chewing gum had the possible side effect of bloating from swallowing too much air. (I looked it up.) Or maybe I ate too much broccoli, which could be gaseous. (I looked that up too.) Either way, I couldn't deal with a large, protruding stomach. The thought depressed me.

By the time I said good-bye to Curtis and my brother and returned to Singapore with my parents, I couldn't shake my growing depression. My circumstances had improved. Mom was home. So why the increased depression? My parents thought my change in mood had to do with missing my brother—that and carrying on a long-distance relationship with a great guy who happened to live in Denver, halfway around the world. I kept asking my mother about my midsection.

"Mom, can you see this?"

"Yes. I've seen that look in a *National Geographic* magazine. You need to eat."

My mother was now aware of my decreased appetite and blamed the depression. She offered an observation about malnutrition and its effects on the body, including a bloated abdomen. She advised me again to eat more and to quit chewing so much gum.

One day while shopping for lingerie, I came across something curious.

"Mom, what's this?"

"That's a corset, honey. You don't need a corset."

"Mom, this could help me. Look. It covers here, where I feel bloated."

I asked if I could at least try it on just to see. She hesitated but agreed and followed me into the dressing room. I held the front while she wrestled with the fasteners on the back. She paused and considered my reflection in the mirror.

"Corinne, you need to take this off."

"No! Mom, do you see what this does for me?"

I felt snug and secure. It supported my frame and added warmth. She couldn't deny that the contraption pulled in my gut, improved my posture, and relieved my anxiety.

"Corinne, this goes against my better judgment as well as what I'm trying to teach you. You are beautiful without this."

"Mom, I'll feel like I can eat more if I don't feel bloated. I really think it's just the broccoli and the gum. Please let me get it."

Every morning before school I'd ask Mom to help me with my undergarment. And every morning she'd ask questions about my nutrition and my weight. This was our morning ritual: she'd notice my bones sticking out, inspect the loose skin on my back, and comment on my deteriorating muscle mass. She'd rub her fingers in a circular motion over each of my vertebrae and ask me if it hurt. One morning, she noticed a slight bruise on my tailbone.

"Corinne, did you fall?"

"No, Mom. But lately it does hurt sometimes when I sit down too long."

"There's a bruise on your neck, too."

Mom said she would call and make an appointment with the doctor.

The doctor checked my weight and drew some blood. He said I looked healthy, but he could refer me to a specialty clinic if I kept losing weight. Mom assured him I would make some changes. I couldn't afford to have my mother taking away my corset and making me eat. There had to be a way to negotiate a win-win.

By the second semester of my junior year, students took stands on their identities and declared their beliefs. Some of my good friends came out of the closet. I still loved them. Would they love me if they knew some of my secrets? Would they make fun of me if they knew I wore a corset? Would they accept me if they knew why? Who was I, anyway? Unsure about so many things, I knew where I stood on food and health.

Mom wouldn't support me as a vegetarian. The term would raise a red flag. However, she did share my love for animals. I thought I might be able to get away with a nutritional stand against harming animals, but it couldn't be extreme. Mom might agree to that.

I informed her of the alarming knowledge I'd gained about the food industry and the unnecessary harm it caused. It wasn't a lie. I was alarmed. The more I researched, the more appalled I became at the handling of the meat that made its way to our table. I thought of a compromise we might reach: I'd eat fish. Mom agreed and so I came to call myself a pescatarian.

I now had a reason not to eat certain foods. I also had support … around my midsection. Mom bought my reasoning. So did I. I thought I'd appeased my mother, but the voice behind the truce wasn't mine at all. Whatever it was, the voice growing inside my head had taken on a form and a power far beyond my ability to contain it.

A friendly, borderline-flirtatious person morphed into an aloof, sometimes reclusive creature. My trademark big hug with a loud, over-the-top "Hi!" became a pat on the back with a shallow one-liner salutation—a tactic to conceal the synthetic shell underneath my shirt. I didn't want to invite questions, but questions came all the same.

"Why do you eat the same thing all the time?"

"How come we don't see you in the caf like we used to?"

"Why are you wearing a sweatshirt?"

I started wearing the sweatshirt for three reasons. The temperature felt cooler than I remembered at the equator, it added layering to hide my corset, and it belonged to Curtis. It was easy to see the sweatshirt didn't belong to me; the dark-blue material swallowed me. It had the name of my boyfriend's summer camp on it. I told those who asked I wore it because I missed him.

It angered me that people called me out on my peculiar habits, the sweatshirt being one of those. The irony strikes me now: what drew me in as a lifestyle adopted partly to gain attention soon directed me to crave isolation. I began to wonder who was in charge— the voice or me.

Toward the end of that school year, I realized I no longer placed myself in an environment where I could be tempted to eat or questioned by my friends. Paranoia played a part in my daily routine. I avoided the cafeteria altogether, choosing study time instead. I scheduled outings with friends before or after meals. I blamed my mom. She became my imaginary strict parent as I made up excuses for having to miss or cancel plans I'd agreed to without fully considering their implications.

I couldn't go to movies; it would be too easy to get distracted and grab a handful of popcorn. There would be no shopping; I didn't want to risk my friends discovering my corset. Sleepovers? Definitely no. I couldn't risk midnight group munchies and having to explain the corset. My thoughts, actions, and motives submitted to this thing inside me, molding my world into a smaller, safer place.

I was safer, but not safe, because I never found complete security, even in my isolation. The voice bullied me, oppressed me, made me feel guilty. It compelled me, saturated me, seduced me.

My sickness drew me to itself, and I didn't even know its identity yet—not the term for it, anyway. It offered control over my food and over my environment. It would never leave me or abandon me. It promised me success. It said I could analyze techniques, conduct research, and achieve goals. I could trust this voice, guiding me every step of the way. And our next goal? Double digits on the scale.

Dad became more active in figuring out what in the world was going on with me. He and my mother sat me down one night to voice their concern. They'd watched my eating habits drastically change and narrow over the last few months, and they wanted it to stop. Mom said she intended to sit with me during breakfast and dinner to make sure I ate. My parents made an appointment with a counselor, who diagnosed me with depression. *Seriously?* I could have told them that one. Mom and Dad decided an emotional gift might lift my spirits.

Breathing Space

My heart raced as I saw Curtis striding toward the baggage claim belt. I could tell he strained to control his gait. The glass wall—the only thing standing between me and the boyfriend I hadn't seen in months—frustrated me. Midnight came and went, but my excitement overrode fatigue. I studied Curtis as the luggage belt teased us, making us wait. His broad shoulders sported a backpack. His hair was cut short. He held a gallon-size water jug in his hand. My legs kept fidgeting. He kept waving. Finally, he grabbed his bag and passed through the glass doorway. We bound into each other's arms and remained immotile until my parents chimed in to say hello.

Welcome to my life. The moments I live for. A holiday from my consuming darkness. Curtis—my refuge, my rest, and the reason for my sanity. The moment we embraced, I could see clearly. My heart calmed. A sense of order filled my spirit. If the voice inside me had something to fear, it would be this—a love that had staked its claim before my illness.

We followed Mom into the house and on into Corbin's room. I hadn't been in my brother's room since he left—almost a year ago. The slight scent of vanilla had replaced the smell of sweat and deodorant. I noticed a candle glowing on top of my brother's built-in study shelf, illuminating the image of a shirtless, muscular giant—a framed poster from the movie *300* hanging on the wall next to his bed. Resting on the corner of the comforter were two bath towels and a basket full of snacks. Mom told Curtis to help himself in the kitchen. She said that iced lemon tea, his favorite, could be found in the fridge, bottom shelf. With that, she bid us goodnight and turned to go upstairs, but then reverted her gaze and said to us both, "Just remember you two. There's one strict rule in this house: Respect that ring."

On the ride to the airport, Daddy had pointed out how much he loved me, trusted me, and valued me as a daughter. He reminded me of the day he'd given me a purity ring, sometime after my twelfth birthday. He recalled our conversation—a mutual promise between the two of us. He had vowed to protect me and to provide for me; I had promised to keep my virginity in tact until I got married. The ring was something I treasured. I proudly wore the symbol, personally designed by my father to reflect a version of his wedding ring. Wearing the ring was a way I could make my parents proud of me.

I'd assured Mom and Dad that Curtis and I understood the expectations: that once we arrived home, Curtis and I would talk only for a short while and then I would turn in; that I would sleep in my own room, upstairs next to Mom and Dad's; that I had school the following morning and needed to be fresh and ready for the day. I intended to follow every detail. I wanted to make sure my parents remained confident in their trust of me and that they remained open to continued visits in the future.

But once Curtis and I were alone, there was no way I could sleep—not upstairs, not with Curtis so close. Corbin's bed was so comfortable, and the smell of my boyfriend so sweet. I snuggled my nose as close as I could to the skin on his neck. I breathed in his essence and listened while his deep voice massaged my ears. I found rest in his arms, and for the first time in months, I slept soundly.

The following morning, I was up and dressed before Mom came out of her room. Curtis and I were excited to get to school. We walked my usual route— each step provided an injection of essential nutrients that had been missing in my emotional diet. It had been almost a year since he had asked if we could try to make our relationship work. I texted Donut and told her we were on her street. And sure enough, not long after my text, I heard her yell. Donut and Curtis ran toward each other. She jumped and he lifted her with ease. They hugged. I watched him and took in the details. His biceps. His eyes closed tight. His smile. Seeing Curtis in a place he loved so much and with friends he'd made during his short stay here left me giddy. I realized I'd do anything to see him that happy.

The three of us continued the short walk to school, passing people here and there who recognized the exchange student who came and left and came back again. The warning bell rang. We briefly kissed and I forced myself to head for class while Curtis took off to catch up with old friends and teachers. I sat at my desk and tried to focus. The Morning Show appeared on the video feed in our classroom. News and events for the day highlighted the upcoming prom.

Guys had outdone themselves this year, asking their dates to the prom in creative, sometimes outlandish ways: skits in the cafeteria, spelling out "Prom?" on the field, dressing up in costumes and making fools of themselves in front of cheering crowds. Most guys were smart and confirmed the reply before asking. A few were not so lucky. I asked about the color of someone's dress when I thought I heard a familiar voice on the monitor above me.

"Corinne, look!" came a voice from behind.

Curtis' image monopolized the screen. The classroom fell silent.

"Hey, everyone. My name's Curtis Alexander, and you may remember me cuz I was a transfer student at SAS last year, second semester. The reason why I'm on here today is because I'm about to ask the most beautiful …"

My heart began to race.

"… gorgeous, just amazing, indescribable girl at SAS to prom. However, it's a bit intimidating, so I recruited some of my friends to help me out. So here goes."

Curtis always found ways to make me love him more, even when I thought it wasn't possible to fall any further.

The video began with guys and girls decked out in gym clothes, running around a track and chanting. I recognized the familiar setting of Curtis' high school. A series of shots followed as a few of his friends added phrases to the chant started by the students on the track—a poem I gathered he'd written about us.

"We've got each other.
That I swear.
Apart a distance,
Some won't dare.
The one I want
Is only thee …"

The screen then flashed to Zazzy, who initiated an invitation, "Corinne, will you go to prom …"

Bubbly, enthusiastic Zazzy! I loved that Curtis had included her.

Next on the screen came Curtis with the final two words: "with me?"

If I had died right then, I would have been whole. My life would have led to this moment when I, the princess, and he, my prince, became that classic tale passed down to future generations.

The video faded to black. Curtis burst through the door of the classroom and approached me, holding one red rose. I sprang up and ran toward him, but he put out his arm and gently pushed me back. He tilted his head and smiled.

"There's more."

How could there possibly be more? I stole a glance around the room while Curtis unfolded a piece of paper. Girls were holding their hands up to their mouths. Guys nodded as if taking mental notes. He began to read something he'd written for me.

For me? This isn't me. This could not be me. I am not standing here, and this is not my life. How could this be happening to me of all people? I didn't deserve this. Not this. Not him. And yet, right there and then, I was the luckiest girl on the planet. And I knew it. After Curtis finished reading, he looked up and saw confusion on my face. I wasn't quite sure how to respond. My hands, covering my mouth, remained frozen in place.

He embraced me and picked me up and held me there as I etched the memory into eternal places.

The following day was a blur. Curtis visited with friends. He stopped by to see his aunt and uncle. For me, nails, makeup, and hair dominated the day. The busy schedule omitted food. Mom asked if she could pick up lunch, but I told her I was saving my appetite for dinner. I'd mentally prepared all week for this special night. I'd counted each calorie and ate as little as possible. I worked out twice as hard in the gym at our club. Now I felt I could reward myself. One meal out with friends. One night off from that pestering voice inside me. I determined to let loose and enjoy the upcoming event.

I sat in the salon at the American Club while a hairstylist curled my long, blond strands and partially pinned them to my head. He added a few small, fresh white and yellow orchids during the styling to complement the orange, red, and yellow splashes of print on my long, black, satin dress. At home, Mom helped me into my corset, adjusting it down to hide it under my scoop back dress. I noticed she no longer struggled with the fasteners. The corset's grip now had a little give to it. I heard some of my friends enter downstairs. Soon our apartment would be filled with chatter. Parents would take pictures for memory boxes to be reviewed a lifetime from now. I wondered what I'd be like then.

I came down the stairs to see friends, parents—and Curtis. We locked eyes like we were the only ones in the room. When I reached him, he placed his hand on my back and gently pulled me to him.

"You're beautiful," he whispered in my ear.

We exchanged a matching yellow-rose corsage and boutonniere and posed on the balcony while Mom took photos. When he again placed his hand on my back he let it slide down my satin dress.

"What's that?" he asked.

I looked at him as if I didn't understand the question.

"What are you wearing? Under the dress?"

"It's a corset."

I didn't want to give away too much information.

"Corinne, I want to feel you, not this."

Mom took some candid shots while we talked. Then she asked us to look at her for a few more posed photos. I welcomed the intermission. I had to think. The corset protected me, but so did Curtis. I would be safe with him. And I wanted to feel his hand softly brushing against my dress without interference from my stupid undergarment. Of course I would take it off.

"Curtis, I'll be right back, okay? Just give me a minute."

I slowly walked by my mother and whispered in her ear.

"Mom, I need you upstairs."

She followed me, saying hellos to our guests as she walked by, asking if they needed another drink or something more to eat.

We walked up the stairs and into my room. I shut the door behind us.

"Help me take this off," I said as I reached for the zipper underneath my arm.

"Why, honey? What's wrong?

"Curtis. He doesn't want me to wear this thing," I said as I tugged at the corset.

"Oh, thank God," she replied.

"Mom!"

"Well ..."

The corset was off, the dress back on.

"Do I look okay, Mom?"

"Even more beautiful now."

She pulled me close and told me not to worry.

"You're in good hands, sweetheart. You're with friends and a boyfriend who adores you. Now go have some fun. Your taxi will be here soon, anyway."

"Thanks, Mom. I needed to hear that."

She was right. My friends cared about me. Curtis cared about me. I was safe. We ate at a rooftop restaurant where I allowed myself to eat salad and steak. When we arrived at the dance I read a sign at the entrance: "A Red Carpet Affair." We played the part, taking group photos while wearing top hats glittered with gold. We danced until my feet hurt and ended the night by rushing home to change into shorts and T-shirts, perfect attire for a water-balloon after-party at a friend's house. We never slept.

Curtis had an early flight to catch. It would take him all of Sunday to travel home for school on Monday. Letting him go was one of the hardest things I had to do. We stood in the airport and held each other. For so many reasons, I wanted him to stay. I needed him to stay.

Sweatshirts and Scales

Curtis's visit gave me a much-needed break from the voice—something I now considered a monster—infiltrating my head. I started living a double life: one with my boyfriend where I felt safe, loved, and able to relax, and one where the disease stood patiently in the shadows until he left, periodically coming out of my subconscious to toy with my maddening mind.

After Curtis left, something struck me. The way he touched me had changed. His hugs were softer. His comments about my figure had changed too. I decided to move my goals up a level, increasing my time and intensity in the gym. I had to get my cute little bubble butt back to its original shape. But no matter how much I lifted, no matter how much I tried, my body did not respond the way I wanted it to.

That confused me. My efforts in the gym should have been paying off in muscle mass. I noticed no increase in muscle mass and definitely no decrease in the size of my tummy. I thought my body had become confused and switched my butt around to my belly. At a loss and with a sense of desperation, I cut out what I thought might be causing the problem. I eliminated milk. Maybe lactose intolerance was to blame. I dropped my midmorning nonfat latte and replaced it with Sugar Free Red Bull.

It's a peculiar experience to watch your body fall apart. I didn't yet know about eating disorders and their consequences; I'd avoided those sites, focusing instead on health and fitness research. I also did not know that as the body learns not to trust the timing of its next meal, it conveniently begins to eat itself.

The color of my skin changed from light pink to a grayish white. Dark circles appeared under my eyes and tiny hairs formed all over my back—my body's way of protecting itself from a lower internal temperature. And curiously, although the hair on my skin increased, the hair on my head began to fall out. I loved my long, blond locks. I was saddened and alarmed as I looked each morning at a brush full of hair, knowing something was wrong.

I continued working out at the club. I even hired a trainer who'd won bodybuilding competitions in the United Kingdom. His intensity and nutritional knowledge led me to believe he could help me. He asked about my diet, especially about my protein intake. He developed a personalized meal plan for me to follow. He said if I wanted to gain muscle, I had to eat more. *Yeah, maybe. After I lose the midsection stuff.*

One day in the gym, I took advantage of an endorphin rush from a heavy workout. I pushed myself. On a high, I threw a medicine ball way up in the air, keeping rhythm with the beat on my play list. Sweat ran down my neck and the backs of my legs. Last set. Four, five, six. All of a sudden I felt a sharp jolt. My wrist gave way. I shook off the pain and finished the set.

Overnight pain and swelling called for a doctor's visit. He took one look at my frame and listened to my pulse for longer than I thought necessary. He asked some questions about my weight and said I needed a cast for my injured wrist. He prescribed special calcium tablets.

My mind raced to the layout of the gym and the equipment requiring a functioning arm: dumbbells, bench press, cable rows, triceps push-downs, rowing, lat pull-downs. *Stupid arm!*

I went home and climbed onto my bed with my one good arm. I checked my pulse. My heart seemed fine to me. I looked at my cast and considered substitute exercises that could build muscle. At least my legs wouldn't be affected. I decided I'd spend more time on the treadmill. I placed two fingers on my neck and held them there; the slow palpitations lulled me to sleep.

Not working out as much meant I had to restrict my diet even more. I took a lot of naps during those days. My body tried to conserve energy. My menses ceased. My posture fell. My abdomen protruded like that of a starving child in Africa. But the kids in Africa had no choice. Was I doing all this by choice?

For sure, restricting offers benefits. The high tops the list.

Control is the underlying foundation for those who restrict their eating. You may ask someone, "What's the most important part of your day?" Drinking water should be somewhere in that answer, but this is so basic that almost no one would think to mention it. Control is water for the anorexic.

The high is what I assume heroin is for an addict or what repeatedly turning a light switch on and off is for the person suffering from obsessive-compulsive disorder. It motivates like no other. Determined and tenacious, it cannot be swayed by opinion or fact. Facts are irrelevant. The number on the scale is all that matters.

I weighed myself every day, sometimes several times a day. Entering the bathroom and stepping on the scale got my blood pumping. Approaching the small white platform block and considering my training, my confidence turned to apprehension as I wondered if I'd put enough effort into preparing for the event.

My bathroom offered a private arena where I could measure my success (or failure). In my head the voices chanted. Some cheered. Some mocked. But the reward if I won—an injection of adrenaline rushing through my veins—propelled me forward. Most times, I wouldn't be let down.

I'd step on the scale and close my eyes. I'd pray. The high I experienced at that moment alone committed me to the process. Every time the number decreased, I breathed in relief. I could hear accolades from my mind's cheering section. This is where I shined. This is where I found success.

My achievements in the bathroom directed most of my daily routine, but the disease couldn't gain control of my every thought. My boyfriend stood in the way of that. With every call he made and word he wrote, Curtis slipped around the defenses of my illness and sacked its control centers, disrupting my attacker's progress. I was the ball, tumbling around until one of them picked me up. I sensed Curtis fighting for me.

Only a few weeks were left until our next visit. We were becoming even closer; against all odds and common sense, we'd made this long-distance thing work. Friends talked: "If anyone can make it, Corinne and Curtis can." Our rare and treasured relationship made people believe that young love could actually last.

I asked Mom if our family could stay part of the summer in a hotel in Denver. That way I could see Curtis more often. My mother agreed on the condition that I'd talk to someone about my growing fear of eating certain foods and that I'd try to gain weight. I agreed.

We'd both come to the conclusion that I had something called *orthorexia*, an unhealthy obsession with eating healthy food. At least that was the only term that came close to describing the gravitational pull of my eating habits. I ate what I thought were regular meals with snacks in between, but few dishes comforted me—those with clearly listed ingredients and fat content. If listed ingredients included oil, I'd ask how much and what kind. I'd pick apart salads to confirm their content. I'd rub my finger across the top of a piece of fish, checking its surface. If the selection didn't agree with me or looked suspicious (added butter, sauce, oil), I had an apple in my purse on standby. I ate a lot of apples.

Mom booked a hotel, got a referral for a psychologist, and set her mind to helping me make a healthy weight gain before senior year. I prepared for the trip by researching restaurants in the Denver area. I pulled up menus online, studied the lunch and dinner options, and memorized the calorie and fat content of each item I'd order. I mentally rehearsed how I'd ask for alterations. I thought up excuses to give the wait staff.

"I'm allergic to vegetable oil" was one of my favorites. I'd be ready with suggestions when the time came to choose a place to eat.

Summer flew by. I took a defensive driving course and practiced my skills navigating downtown to my psychologist's office. Mom went with me. I could tell she enjoyed the visits; she'd listen as the psychologist asked me to try to identify the voice harassing me, to give it a name. I tried. I even threw in the name of someone who'd bullied me in middle school. Maybe bullying had stunted my emotional growth. Maybe the bully was my monster. I just couldn't make the explanation stick. It didn't ring true for some reason. The voice in my head sounded more like an it than a him or a her.

I'd feel exhausted by the end of each appointment. Mom rewarded my efforts with a trip to Whole Foods. I'd spend a lot of time reading the ingredient lists at the salad bar. Finding foods I could eat there comforted me: kale salad, soups, fresh veggies. Whole Foods, after all, meant healthy eating.

Curtis worked during the summer. On the days we saw each other, we'd play like kids at recess—riding bicycles, swinging at the park, wandering the grounds at his old high school. One late afternoon after a day together, Curtis and I returned to the Alexander home to find a somber scene. His parents had called a family meeting and invited me to join. The topic: whether Curtis should play football his senior year. Curtis loved the game, but he'd suffered several concussions, which concerned his family. And me.

I was quiet, sitting in a chair, listening to his aunt, a doctor, discuss what another hit could cost him. My heart broke for Curtis. I knew him. He'd choose the reasonable path. I felt his burden, though, at the prospect of being unable to play a sport he loved or be a part of a team. I wanted so badly to make everything better for him.

We left the house and ended up at Tokyo Joe's—a safe option for me. I could eat the Boulder veggie bowl. No brown rice. No oil. We sat quietly. I was content, knowing I could be there for him.

At the end of that summer I left on a high note. In one short year I'd be back in the States. Curtis and I would be in college, and no matter how far apart our choices might take us, we acknowledged that future flights would be a breeze compared to those that led to and from Singapore.

Corbin reenrolled at SAS. It would be good to have him home. Having my family whole again in a steady environment meant I could go back to the way things were before I got the flu and missed so much school, before my brother started cutting, before he and my mother and my boyfriend all left at the same time. A brand new year meant a brand new start. Everything would be better, which meant I'd no longer need to control something like food. Life was good.

I bounced up the high school steps, positive and upbeat, and ran into Donut. We planned on meeting for lunch in the cafeteria.

Senior year brought with it a feeling I hadn't experienced yet—frenetic, festive, focused. I concentrated on leaving Puppy Love in good hands, while Corbin connected on the football field and with old friends. All was well, or should have been.

I entered the cafeteria.

"Rinney! Come here!" Donut said as she saw me.

I'd expected sitting in the senior section on the top level of the cafeteria to be an exhilarating experience. The top tier was our domain now. Why did I still feel like a freshman? I found the surrounding confidence intimidating. People stood in line to order food. Others sat, ate, and laughed. I looked at all the people and all the food. I couldn't stay there. I thought of an excuse to go.

"Hey, Donut. Something came up with Puppy Love and I've gotta take care of it."

"Aiyo. Thought we were Skyping Curtis. Everyone wants to say hi and to tell him to get back over here."

"Yeah, no kidding! I'll get him on Skype with you soon. Text me later?"

My eating disorder was now acting like a dictator! It didn't seem to matter if life was good or bad. Controlling my food intake had become a compulsive part of the daily routine, and I didn't seem to have any say in it.

My friends must have thought something was up. I often disappeared and made up excuses for why I couldn't go places or do things with them. Or maybe they thought Puppy Love took up most of my time.

Going dancing with Donut seemed to be the only activity that didn't involve having to scramble for ways to make an escape. She loved to dance, and I could do that. The dance clubs didn't even open till late, so I didn't have to worry about food. I'd eat at home then get ready to go out. She and I would dance and laugh at inside jokes and at the guys who tried nonsensical pickup lines like, "What kind of shampoo do you use?"

Out with Donut.

Donut and I also had fun baking together. We'd host Halloween and Valentine's parties at my place. I enjoyed baking for others and frequently brought cakes to school for bake sales and birthdays. I'd spend hours searching the Web and cookbooks for recipes and would whip up my own as well. My brain tried to satisfy itself with anything it could: the act of baking, the smell of sweet and savory.

Like Pavlov's dog, Mom would retrieve her wallet whenever I mentioned food, hoping some aroma would grab my attention and tempt me to ingest something other than what an herbivore might find appealing. But no baked good, no sweet, no savory item could tempt me to cheat on my beloved scale. Sure, I'd lick the batter and smile, commenting in detail on the amazing flavors. I'd ask others if I should add a touch more vanilla to this or cinnamon to that. I might even take a bite for good show, but afterward I would head straight for the fridge and grab a Sugar-Free Jell-O or Vitamin Water Zero to quench any desire that might entice me further.

So why didn't my mother notice my overbaking and undertasting? Why didn't she notice me chugging Vitamin Water instead of enjoying a single cupcake or cookie, even though many times she stood right there in the same kitchen? Why didn't I realize that frantically reaching for Sugar-Free Jell-O warranted a call for help? And why didn't I shudder when I finally reached my goal of weighing below one hundred pounds and realized I couldn't tell anyone? There was something in that scenario that should have caused concern.

Once my weight fell below a hundred pounds, my nutrition became more about sugar-free or fat-free choices. To lose more I had to change more. I acted obsessed. I was obsessed. But I hid my obsession well. I forced myself to go to movies with family or friends. I'd feign excitement ordering popcorn. I'd choose the sweet and salty flavor. We'd sit and share the snack while watching the movie. I'd make it look as though I was eating a fair amount, but I'd chew the smallest bits out of each popped kernel as slowly as I could. I made it a game to see how long I could make one piece of popcorn last. This form of eating not only allowed me to attend movie outings, but let me enjoy the few pieces I did eat.

The cold is what I remember most. I was always cold. Can you imagine being cold when you're living on the equator? My sweatshirt became my safe place, my shelter, my comfort. When I went out, my sweatshirt went with me. When I wasn't wearing my sweatshirt, the hairs on my arms and my back would stand and beckon to be covered.

As my disorder progressed, my memory deteriorated. Dizziness came often. Headaches increased. But no matter my state of health, each afternoon I'd head to the gym for a workout. Nothing and no one interrupted my workout schedule.

My personal trainer had mastered the mechanics of the body. He understood nutrition so well that doctors referred their clients to him. I soaked in everything he had to say. He encouraged me to put on weight, but the only weight I wanted to add was to the metal bar I found harder and harder to lift. He told me about the benefits of protein and muscle. He told me carbs were not my enemy. I learned the positions, the planes, and the mechanics of lifting. I loved it. I got it. Or so I thought. But what he didn't know was that I had something at home I valued even more than his input: my scale. It gave me numbers I could see and immediate feedback I could trust.

Trust. What an interesting concept. People let you down all the time. They say that they love you or that you're a close friend and then they're gone. Families fight and say hurtful things that can never be erased. I know of family members who haven't spoken to each other in years, with bitterness creeping in and taking root in the form of competition or pride, consuming relationships. The thought that sweatshirts and scales were more reliable seemed sensible to me.

A Pendant with a Promise

I put my faith in only one person. Curtis always found ways to lift my spirits and give me the courage I needed to face my days. On Valentine's Day 2011, the doorbell rang. I found a dozen pink roses with a laminated card that read:

> "To: Princess Corinne Weber
>
> Happy Valentine's Day, Angel! I hope these flowers will brighten up your Valentine's Day just like you brighten up every one of my days.
>
> Your OsoPriceCreeper"

I smelled each rose and made a mental note of the one I'd later cut, dry, and press inside my diary. It was flawless, like us. I studied the card and noticed the misspelling: *Price* instead of *Prince*. I chuckled to myself at the idea of someone trying to decode the name while taking the order.

The first two portions of the nickname weren't so strange. *Oso*, or "bear" in Spanish, described the way he hugged me. The celestial pattern Oso held our star. *Prince* was what I had thought the first day he walked into my English class. But *Creeper*?

Creeper. What a way to end a term of endearment. But the word fit our relationship, which ran the gamut from intense romance to corny friendship. *Creeper* emerged from another flower delivery. The arrangement arrived with just my name on a card, no signature. I walked around school all day with the idea of a "creeper" following me. It wasn't until I spoke with Curtis that I learned he'd sent the flowers to say he loved me. I accused him of being my creeper, hence the epithet. He became my OsoPrinceCreeper.

I dashed to the computer to check my e-mail. I couldn't wait to respond. I opened my account to find another e-mail from Curtis—a poem bordered by red hearts.

It was long and descriptive. He wrote about our relationship over the past twenty months. Curtis described himself as a knight—Sir Tristram. And I was the fine and delicate princess he'd dreamed of when he was a small boy. He said I was strong and generous. He said that I made him feel real and that he didn't know who he'd be without me.

I finished reading the poem and didn't consider the "strong" and "generous" parts as much as I zeroed in on the word *delicate*. I determined to remain his delicate princess.

Tristram and Isoude fell in love permanently, passionately, deeply. The two medieval characters are romantic legend, their story intertwined with the story of the Knights of the Round Table. Tristram was strong and able, a skilled archer who was equally talented in the arts. He lived in a world characterized by honor and chivalry. Isoude called love a force as strong as death. But their love wasn't meant to be: Tristram's struggle between his love for the princess and his loyalty to family would become their downfall.

People asked us how in the world we made long distance work. I'd tell them something about our love for each other, but it was more than feeling and commitment. Our relationship's foundation was built on deep friendship, respect, and wanting the best for each other. We spoke with care and tender politeness. We created a time and space that spanned the barriers of distance with stories and dreams. And yes, sometimes I wished I could run to someone nearby on a bad day or when something exciting happened that I wanted to share in person. But we transcended all of that. Curtis was always with me.

Anyone I could have had close to me would never have compared to what we shared. To me, our relationship represented faith—knowing Curtis was walking beside me even though I could not see him, and with every step, sharing my depths of despair as well as my moments of happiness. Sure, loneliness sometimes overshadowed me. But the alternative—to be without him? I'd take loneliness any day. Besides, we always had a plan for the next time we'd see each other.

We had summer and winter breaks. My family returned to Colorado during those times. More often than not, our parents would surprise us with trips in between. My birthday fell around October break, giving me just enough time to spend my seventeenth and eighteenth birthdays with Curtis. His parents allowed him to come to my junior prom. Then, for his senior prom, my parents said they'd send me to Colorado for that.

Friends saw our relationship as a modern day fairy tale. I'd go about my day and sometimes put on my headphones to recharge. I'd select a song Curtis burned to a CD for me as a Christmas gift—"Missing My Baby" by G. Love & Special Sauce. It would be a good day.

Senior prom exceeded my hopes. Seven couples piled into a stretch limo where flashing lights and blaring music set the tone for the night. After the dance at a Denver museum, we took the limo back to the home of one of Curtis' friends where our group changed into matching t-shirts and mismatched bottoms. We then made our way to Curtis' high school where the fun continued. We played carnival games. We ran through the gym and the halls. I felt included, like I'd always been a part of this childhood group of friends. And the party didn't end there.

The high school carnival atmoshphere morphed into a smaller gathering at another home—an all-nighter hosted by the parents of another friend. I never wanted that night to end. I dreaded the sunrise. I thought if I tried hard enough, I could will the sun to remain below the horizon. I needed more time.

Curtis stroked my hair. My back was turned toward him. I focused in on the sounds of slumber from nearby couples.

"Baby, look at me. Corinne, please."

His voice was soft and full of love. I slowly rolled over. He wiped away a lone tear trailing down my cheek.

"Don't cry, baby," he whispered. "Your eyes are too beautiful to hide behind tears."

I looked away.

"How can I not cry?" I asked. "My heart breaks with the thought of leaving you—again. And what if this is the last time? What if this is the last time I'll ever see you, or touch you, or even kiss you?"

Curtis chuckled.

"Corinne, what are you talking about?"

"Curtis, things are changing quickly. Next year we'll be in college."

He put his thumb underneath my chin, lifting it so my eyes locked with his.

"And?" he asked.

I could feel the pounding of my heart.

"And what if you don't want me anymore? What if you want to explore and try new things?"

"You mean try new girls," he answered, his voice now deep and hollow.

"Yes," I replied in a whisper.

My heart sank at the thought of him kissing someone else. More tears rolled down my cheeks.

"Curtis Alexander, if you want or even need to go out and try new things, you need to tell me now. I don't want to lose you. You're the love of my life and I want us to be together, but I love you too much not to let you go—if that's what you want."

I sighed slowly and deliberately and then continued, "Just please do it now because if it's later, it'll kill me."

Curtis grabbed my hands and kissed them.

"Corinne Weber, I've thought about this a lot, and yes, college is a huge step for both of us. I don't know if it's a good thing for us to stay together during college."

I unlocked my eyes from his and braced myself for pain as he continued to speak.

"And I don't know what the future holds for both of us," he said in a softer tone. "But I do know one thing: I know I love you."

I looked up at him with a newfound curiosity. I'd expected the conversation to take a different direction.

"Corinne, you're my princess, my life, and my only love. Without you, my life would be empty. Hold on. I have something for you," he said, sitting up. "I was going to give this to you before you left tomorrow, but something tells me you need it now."

Curtis' hand unfolded, revealing a silver, heart-shaped pendant with wings.

"I made it," he said.

My mouth dropped. My hands moved to cover my heart.

"Corinne, you're my angel and you always will be. I love you with all my heart and soul, and I'm never, ever going to leave you."

The intensity in his eyes matched the fire in my soul, and at that moment I thought we'd never be apart.

I Have What?

T he comfort and happiness flowing from my relationship with Curtis could not evict the monster hanging out in my head. My monster was there to stay—and evolving into something reckless.

Although I'd suffered with anorexia for well over a year, no one had used that term. I'd thought all along my disorder had been orthorexia. Mom thought the same.

The news came to us one day at a consultation with a psychologist who specialized in eating disorders. Mom made the appointment because my weight continued to drop—ninety-four pounds and falling. She'd also taken note of my increased moodiness around mealtime. I think she was fed up with my compulsive behavior.

It was my monster's fault, giving us away by acting out of control and moving too quickly now, making a mess and leaving an obvious trail of rapid weight loss and temper tantrums.

We entered the clinic. I sat down while Mom checked in and retrieved some paperwork. The instructions asked me to write down what I'd eaten during the week. That was easy:

(1) Breakfast: large plate of grilled veggies, no oil, spray-on Bragg's Liquid Aminos
(2) Snack: nonfat latte, gum
(3) Lunch: 4 p.m. at home: grilled veggies, spray-on aminos, Vitamin Water Zero
(4) After workout: whey protein powder with skim milk
(5) Dinner: steamed white fish with steamed veggies; no oil
(6) After-dinner snack: apple, Sugar-Free Jell-O

Mom said I would see a psychologist then visit with a doctor. I reviewed what I wrote down. I confirmed an array of veggies and protein. I'd even added milk back into my diet. I thought the psychologist might ask why I held off on having lunch until late afternoon. Would she think I ate enough? And then I remembered my "blow it day!"

In my research I came across an article that discussed throwing off the body's metabolism to lose weight. It said adding a high-calorie meal to the diet would boost metabolism and cause the body to burn more fat as a result of fluctuating hormone levels. Body builders practiced it. They called it a "cheat meal" or a "blow it day." I'd decided I could eat a cheat meal on Sunday and address the guilt by not eating breakfast or lunch the following day. I'd work out extra hard on Mondays. I could eat and still lose weight! In my mind, I was only following the guidelines for a health-conscious person.

I wrote down what I ate for brunch on Sundays (a recent family tradition at the American Club): cheese, crackers, bread, breadsticks, salmon, wasabi cereal prawns, mango, watermelon, jackfruit, strawberries, red grapes, green grapes, longan, lychee, mangosteen, cheese cake, apple crumble, and white chocolate straws. That should be good enough for the doctor.

Next, the questionnaire asked about my sleep habits. I thought about what to write. I usually went to bed at around 10 p.m. I loved sleeping. I usually dreamed of perfect lives and happy-ever-afters. I could live in that state forever if it weren't for the annoying ringing of my internal alarm clock, which in those days sounded more like an alarm bell. *Four o'clock in the morning! So early!* I'd wake with a jolt and immediately think of breakfast.

I wrote down, "In bed by 10 p.m. Sometimes wake up at 4 a.m. I nap sometimes at school."

The psychologist called me into her office. My mother made a move to follow me but was asked to remain in the waiting room. The psychologist and I talked about my history, my feelings, and my daily menu. It's all a little blurry, but my case notes went like this:

I am writing this down to provide you a summary of our sessions.

21 May 2011. You wanted to regain control over your eating pattern. You felt that the preoccupation with losing weight had led to reduced concentration and energy, frequent mood swings (depression, anger, irritability) and increasing isolation. You wanted to stop the obsessional thinking about food and be able to eat without mentally torturing yourself afterwards and/or exercising compulsively.

You listed the advantages of losing weight—including the "high" from it— although the need to continue doing so seems to be associated with the fears of reverting back to normal eating habits. You fear that you will lose control and gain all the weight back. You are not confident in your ability to moderate eating and do not trust your body's ability to metabolize food (i.e., if you ate something new or different to what you

are used to, it will show up as weight
gain the next day). There is also guilt
whenever you eat something and the
anticipation of negative reactions from
other people if you gained a little weight.

She took my weight and height and brought my
mom in for the wrap-up.

"Well, in Corinne's case, I'll need to see her twice
a week before she leaves for the States. We'll also get
her on some medication to ease the anxiety caused
from increasing her daily caloric intake. For anorexics,
it's a hard road. Some recover and some do not."

*Wait ... what did she say? Did she use the term
'anorexic'?* Swimming, my mind searched for excuses.
But I have orthorexia. I like to eat and I eat a lot! I looked
at my mom and tried to make her read my mind.
*You've seen what's on my plate. Heaps of healthy stuff! I did
the research. That's what I do—research! I even have blow-it
days! Anorexics restrict, while orthorexics aren't focused on
the quantity of the food but on the quality. That's me! I'm
healthy! Don't you see me in the gym all the time? I drink
protein shakes after a workout, and I eat white fish for dinner.
Big deal!* The conversation played out like a silent film
inside my head, my mouth refusing to participate, too
tired to fight.

I was sent home with an eating diary sheet to
record my daily intake of food. I said I'd try to add

more variety. What I really wanted to say was how dumb I thought the staff members were and how stupid my mom was for buying their garbage.

I dutifully logged my nutritional intake on that Saturday, May 21. Sunday followed. Blow-it day! I picked up a different sheet with a line down the middle of two labeled columns: "What I Would Lose by Gaining Weight" and "What I Would Gain by Gaining Weight." I listed four more thoughts in column two than in column one. I considered column one again. What would I lose by gaining weight? I wrote thoughtfully for a few minutes. Then I put the paper down and never wrote in the diary again.

This wasn't working. The doctor didn't have the answers I needed to stop the downward progression before heading to college in seven short weeks. I had to go to Chapman. My parents wouldn't dare let me go if I revealed all the alarms sounding in my body and my mind. The disease now had full command of my systems.

I stepped on the scale. Another 0.2-pound loss pinged another distress signal. SOS. I Googled "BMI calculator," put in my weight (ninety-three pounds) and my height (five foot six), placed the mouse over the highlighted blue box containing the oh-so-ironic words "Are you overweight?"—and paused. I considered my protruding stomach and answered in the affirmative. Click.

"Your Body Mass Index (BMI) is 15.0. This means your weight is within the Underweight range. Your current BMI is lower than the recommended range of 18.5 to 24.9. To be within the right range for your height, you should weigh between 115 lbs / 52.1 kg and 154 lbs / 69.8 kg."

Well, first of all, the results didn't say anything about an "unhealthy" range or a "must get help" range. The other end of the spectrum is more obvious: "obese" or "morbidly obese." However, no scale I'd seen addressed "morbidly underweight." Furthermore, 115 was a big number. That my weight should start at that number had to be an overstatement or a mistake. I could never get to 115 and wouldn't want to. And what about that range? Thirty-nine pounds of leeway for the "normal" weight range based on my height? *Are you kidding me?* I suspected a big conspiracy. The numbers made no accounting for frame, bone size, or muscle tone. I made a mental note: those who make up standards and call themselves experts have no idea what they're talking about.

Looking thinner than ever in my graduation pictures, I went out and danced the night away on another adrenaline high, saying good-bye to friends and the manic Singaporean lifestyle. From the States, I'd dutifully keep my promise to continue sessions via Skype with the psychologist. I wasn't about to mess up my future.

Graduation day with Corbin.

By the second week of June, the medication kicked in, allowing some reprieve from the incessant chatter in my head. Having graduated and moved back to the States, I shuffled from one relative's house to another. I celebrated living back in the land of my youth. I also celebrated the fact that I was no longer immersed in a city of walking sticks—Americans, in general, were fuller-figured than Asians.

I added a little variety back into my diet. I had to. News of my illness had spread through the family grapevine. My relatives were on high alert and ready to serve. Uncle Carter offered me his custom-made pancakes packed with bananas or blueberries or whatever he felt like adding on any given Saturday morning. He wouldn't take no for an answer. Grandmother made her summer strawberry shortcake topped with whipped cream. Mom took me out for frozen yogurt. I ate small bites here and there, but the food didn't taste good and it was hard to swallow. Sometimes I'd cry while I ate. Mom would put her hand on my leg and whisper in my ear that I was okay and that the voice in my head was lying to me. So I ate. I wanted to please my family as well as my psychologist. I had a goal to reach and a university to attend.

Scales were hard to find. I now know few people place them in the guest bathroom. So they were out of sight but not out of mind. When the call came from Singapore for the weekly update, I found an excuse to ask if I could weigh myself. I hoped I could give a good report. But not that good.

I stepped on the scale. Two pounds! I quickly stepped off and tried again. Sure enough, I'd gained two pounds in one week! At that rate, I'd put on the freshman fifteen before setting foot on campus. No way. Not a chance. How could it be that easy to put on weight? I wasn't eating that much, certainly not as much as others who ate with me. I'd made sure of that. I thought maybe I'd gained half a pound—a large amount I had prepared myself to face. But two?

The Skype call went well—on the other end of the screen, anyway. The psychologist told me to stay the course and reiterated the importance of a food diary as well as a journal.

"But how is that possible? How could I gain two pounds in just one week?"

"Every scale is different. And you've been traveling. Water retention is probably part of the weight gain, but remember that increasing your caloric intake and putting on some healthy weight is your goal here. Keep a record of food and feelings, and we'll talk next week."

I hung up and sat stunned as Mom reassured me. She praised me for my progress. She said she'd noticed my face looked less "gaunt." What I heard: my cheekbones were less defined, I was fat and ugly, and the "progress" I'd made was a complete failure. What if I did "stay the course" like my psychologist asked? What if I continued to gain weight? What if I passed a hundred—that mile marker that made me feel I'd accomplished something of value? What would define me if I got better? Losing defined me. Being thin was my thing. What would be my thing if I started gaining?

I decided to follow my psychologist's instructions—as far as the record keeping, anyway. I wrote down everything I ate, drank, and chewed. (Yes, I even wrote down gum.) I kept the lists on sticky notes, on torn pieces of paper, on napkins. I recorded everything. I had to make sure I could lose again.

By the following week, I'd lost more than I thought. Back down to ninety-three. Thank God. This time the call went better on my end, at least until my psychologist announced the "new plan."

> "Case Notes via Skype call:
> 14 June 2011
> New plan (1,800 calories per day)
> -Breakfast (300)
> -Snack (200)
> -Lunch (500)
> -Snack (200)
> -Dinner (300)
> -Bedtime snack (300)"

All I saw were numbers. Loads and loads of numbers. The calories for lunch alone were more than I sometimes consumed in a whole day. According to the new plan, Mom had to supervise my food intake. She could add calories at the end of each day if there was a deficit. The psychologist told me to inform my mother about my weight loss. The new plan of 1,800 calories per day was intended to help me gain back one of the lost pounds in a week; failing to do so by the following Skype appointment would activate my parents' alternative plan for me. The psychologist said she would follow-up with Mom by email.

Mom and Dad were now talking about in-house treatment, which meant delaying my freshman year of college. I did not want that plan to kick in. They wouldn't do that, would they? College was expected as the next step in life's natural progression. Dad made it clear that financial support came with the understanding that we would continue our schooling. Would he forgo the opportunity to send his daughter to college? Was I that sick?

We came home and Mom took a picture of me in my underwear so I could see what ninety-three pounds looked like. She asked me to study the photo and tell her what I saw. I glanced at the picture, but I didn't want to talk about it. She wouldn't understand. I didn't even understand, not really. How could I explain to her that I viewed muscle and weight as separate issues? I wanted muscle. I wanted proportion. I wanted to look pretty. But if I told her that what I saw in the photo was that I needed to add muscle, she would respond that I had to put on weight in order to do that. I didn't see it that way. What really stuck out to me in the picture were my big hips. I also saw a waist that could be smaller. My tummy could attest to that. What I saw was not pretty. I had to get to the gym.

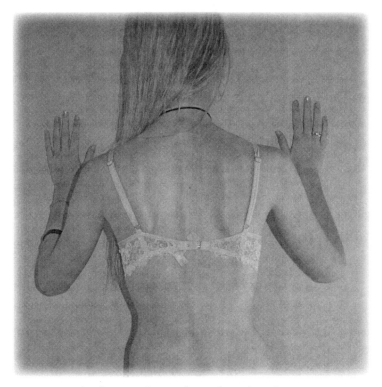

A photo taken of me that day. I was
ninety-three pounds and still dropping.

The Last Time

I'd confided in Curtis, telling him about my diagnosis. He wasn't surprised. He said he already knew. *He already knew? How did he already know? How could he have known something about me that I didn't? What else did he know? And why hadn't he said anything?* He expressed his confidence in me as well as his gratitude for the help I'd received. He said we'd get through this together. He looked forward to helping me eat new things. I flew to Denver with my family, excited yet feeling a bit vulnerable.

Now that he understood the extent of my condition, Curtis tried to get me to eat by taking me to some of his favorite places. He tried to encourage me by saying, "Let's split a burger" or "How about dessert?" But each time, I'd meet his offers with, "I think I'll just get a salad." One day he gave me an ultimatum I couldn't refuse.

"Come on," he said in his playful voice that tempted me every time.

"Where are we going?" I said with a laugh.

"It's a surprise."

I smiled and hopped into the passenger seat. We exited his driveway and cruised along familiar windy roads. He then pulled into an unfamiliar parking lot. I looked around to see several different restaurants.

"Okay, Curtis. What's this about? Where are we?"

Curtis parked and then looked at me and smiled.

"We're at Cinnabon."

We'd fantasized about sharing this gooey treat, but that was before. I'd never thought it would happen, especially now. He didn't expect me to actually eat a cinnamon roll, did he?

He must have seen the fear on my face because he grabbed my hands and said, "Corinne, I love you. But I can't keep doing this."

A chill rushed through me as he continued.

"If you're not willing to get better, if you're willing to give up, I can't be around to see that. Show me you're prepared to at least try to get better. I won't leave you for battling anorexia, but I won't stay and watch you wither away."

My eyelids were heavy and could not lift to meet his, so I looked at the ground, weighing my priorities and fighting my thoughts. My anorexic mind told me he didn't care about me. *If he can't accept you for who you are, good riddance. You should just leave him.*

But I knew Curtis cared. I knew he loved me, and I wasn't about to throw away a great relationship over a cinnamon roll. I slowly lifted my head to meet his eyes and whispered, "Okay … Okay, I'll do it."

Curtis smiled again and reached over to hug me from across his seat. As he pulled away, he kissed me and said, "We can do this together."

Each step toward the door felt as if I were walking through cement. I wanted to run away, but I sensed backing out now would mean the end of our relationship. We stood in line. Curtis held my hand. As we sat down with the little box, I saw only one fork and knife at the table.

"Aren't we gonna share it?" I asked.

Curtis looked at me and said, "I'll have a little, but this is for you."

I panicked. He expected me to eat the whole thing!

"I can't. Curtis, I can't!"

He rubbed my hands and said, "Corinne, I believe in you. I'm right here and I'm not going anywhere. Here, I'll take the first bite."

Curtis cut off a big chunk of the roll. It oozed with icing. He eased it into his mouth, and chewed. I saw delight make its way across his face. *If only it were that easy.*

Then he cut a piece for me and held the fork in front of me. My throat initiated a gag reflex, defending itself against the threat of a foreign object. My head started pounding. The voice amplified to a sound louder than a siren.

The first bite assaulted my taste buds. The sensation of sugar and butter. My stomach turned against me, wanting to retch. My monster abused me: *It's a trick! Why would he do this to you, knowing how much it hurts you? You'll get fat from this. He'll leave you tomorrow. Just wait. You think your stomach's big now? Wait till tonight when you can't sleep. You'll pay, Corinne.*

I'd never experienced torture like this before. I thought the voices were bad, but this exceeded mental abuse. I could feel the fat swishing around in my mouth. It was all I could do to swallow what I imagined as greased-filled pustules making their way into my bloodstream and congregating in the lining of my expanding gut. I had no doubt the following morning would find me as large as a whale. Tears flushed my eyes.

It took me a long time to finish that Cinnabon. Curtis had five bites. I had the rest. As we left the popular chain of sweets, I realized my mind was shackled to the store. Its lingering offensive scent trailed behind me and wouldn't leave me alone. I decided never to go there again. I held my tummy and shook as the idea of blowing up consumed me. I understood my boyfriend was trying to help, but it was too much, too soon. I felt attacked, and so I mentally retreated. I ate for Curtis. I did it for our relationship. But the punishment would have to fit the crime. I'd have to pay for what I'd done. No food for the following two days. I didn't know any other way to calm the sea of violence roiling inside my head.

Curtis and I continued texting every day and saw each other when we could. His work as a camp counselor kept him busy, while I prepared for my freshman year by getting a head start on a book for a class on leadership. The required reading included an account of Sir Ernest Shackleton's failed trans-Antarctic expedition and how his leadership brought every member of his twenty-eight-man crew back alive. They suffered through hunger and cold and odds working against them. I could relate.

On one of Curtis' nights off from work, my mom and I drove to Denver to meet him, his sisters, and his dad for dinner at Sweet Tomatoes. We found a table and made our way to the buffet stations. Mom followed behind me, encouraging me to choose some carbs. When we all sat down, I asked the girls about their week; they'd attended a session at the camp where their brother worked.

"Curtis has a camp crush," one of the girls said, giggling over the spilled milk.

Curtis looked at me reassuringly.

"It's nothing," he said.

"He had to choose," one of his sisters said.

They were only ten. I wasn't about to hold anything against them. As the girls continued their stories, however, I recalled my dad's relationship advice to Corbin one night while we all sat on the patio at the ranch. He said other women should never be an option, not even in jest. His lesson about temptation and how it usually begins as something innocent now gave me goose bumps.

My attention turned back to the table as Curtis glanced at the muffin I'd pushed aside. His father followed the girls' narrative with tales about how some camp kids come back as counselors and end up marrying each other. *Why would he say that? And why now?* I'd been up to the camp with Curtis and loved the look on his face as he escorted me around the site. I didn't want my feelings to change about him being there without me.

Curtis continued to divide his off-days between his family and me, making the effort to drive more than two hours each time to see me. One morning he left the ranch early enough to be at work by eight. When he arrived at the camp he realized he'd misread his schedule. He didn't have to be back until later that night. Curtis called me, hardly able to contain his excitement.

"I have the day off! Can I come back up?" he asked.

Curtis drove another two hours back to the house to spend the rest of the day with me. I ran to meet him as his car approached. He couldn't get to my open arms fast enough. Every time was like this. We'd run and embrace each other like we'd missed out on the grandest gift of being in each other's presence. The only drawback to our visits involved his parents' phone calls. They were concerned about Curtis missing out on time with his family and friends. I dismissed their complaint with thoughts of how little time I spent in town—a few weeks twice a year. They got him all year long.

The day Curtis drove back up to the house, there came another call from his parents. He held the phone for what seemed an eternity. He said only "yes" and "I heard you." The precious moments we lost made me question the monologue on the other end of the line. What could be so dire? He hung up, obviously upset.

"What did they say?"

"My parents wanted to know if I had made the decision to stay with you during college."

I remained absolutely still.

"I said yes," he assured me.

His words rang with determination.

He continued, "But they have some rules we'll have to follow."

I wondered what I'd done wrong. *Why didn't they like me?* I'd supported Curtis in whatever he wanted to do. I'd encouraged him to take girls on dates to school parties when I couldn't be there. I'd celebrated his choice to go to a school in the Midwest even though it was far from Los Angeles and Chapman. I'd remained quiet in family matters involving something as serious as his health. We'd both been excited to soon live only hours from each other instead of half a world away.

But maybe none of that was good enough for his parents. Maybe they knew more about my sickness than they'd let on. They'd never asked and I never offered. If they had discovered my illness, maybe they considered me damaged goods. If that was the reason they opposed our relationship, I couldn't fault them for that. I wouldn't be a suitable match for their son.

Sitting at the kitchen table early one August morning, my mother and I were planning our fourteen-hour road trip from Vail to Los Angeles when I spotted movement outside.

"Mom," I said quietly. "Look!"

A doe and her fawn stood beyond the back patio, staring at us. This wasn't an unusual occurrence at the ranch, but this morning I noticed the remarkable similarities in the two pairs staring back at each other. The doe was protective, assessing the danger. The fawn awaited a signal of distress. I watched as the doe's ears shifted, gathering data from all directions. She then lowered her head and nibbled on some nearby ground cover. The fawn followed her lead. I thought of my own mother—so much like the protective doe. The idea of college could be exhilarating, and yet I could see clouds of doubt cross her mind. She knew I was stubborn and determined. But did she think I could do this? Could I go to college with a chronic illness?

"Corinne, what do you think?" she asked.

I snapped back into planning mode. *What was the question? Oh yeah, got it.*

"Yeah, I'd like to see that."

Cirque du Soleil's *Viva Elvis* seemed appropriate for our stopover in Vegas. I'd heard stories that my maternal grandfather had looked and sung like the King. Mom was quite fervent in her enthusiasm, attempting to redirect my introspective state toward the glitz and glamour that awaited us in the City of Lights.

After we settled on the entertainment, she turned her focus to meal planning. I'd have a hard time resisting Cracker Barrel's breakfast for dinner. A tradition since I'd been a little girl, the country store always tempted my timid fingers with old-time candies and trinkets. Mom must have known the thick French toast with warm maple syrup would have a good shot at overriding my restrictive measures. I'd worry about the guilt later. Mom found a location for the restaurant in St. George, Utah, about eight hours into the trip. Perfect timing for dinner. Road trip planned. Time to pack.

The land at the ranch is dotted with aspen groves. September would come soon with her palette and brush, painting the treetops buttercup and turning the valley into a canvas of textured artistry. The contrast of the yellow leaves against the evergreens sparks majestic reflection in the hardest of hearts. I could always take refreshment in creation, from the animals crossing my path to the sound of these aspens while I cleared the brush.

On an early afternoon, Corbin and I walked the land, picking up cut dead logs and loading them onto Grandpa's Gator. After each load, we'd haul the piles to a dump site on the back edge of the property where we'd empty the contents of the trailer. Then we'd take a rest or play a round of paintball. The hard work made us feel good. I perceived a marked difference in my brother—his calm manner in loading and unloading the logs, the gentle assurances he gave when my paint gun jammed, the way he paused and looked out over the valley. I think the land had the same effect on him as it did on me.

I'd miss Corbin but I was so proud that he'd found the way through his internal struggle. And now he was heading off to college. The keloid scars on his upper-left arm served as fading reminders of a war once waged against him. I guess he could say he encountered a bear, but he didn't seem to mind the evidence of his journey, wearing revealing tank tops that announced a life already marked by intense pain.

I remembered hearing a story about a youth pastor who had a large following. All inked up and wearing large gauges in his drooping earlobes, he'd caused quite a stir with conservatives in and around his profession. But the kids loved it. They came to him with real problems because he was real as well, displaying signs of conflict between what the world expected and what Jesus might have accepted. I thought about Corbin and his approachable nature. He talked about wanting to return to the wilderness camp as a counselor. I thought that would suit him. I also wondered about the rules of religion. It's a well-known fact that Jesus hung out with prostitutes and tax collectors. I wondered if maybe Jesus would hang out with someone as messed up as me if He were walking around today.

Time to say good-bye. The following day, Curtis came up to the house to spend the afternoon and night. The plans included introducing him to some of my relatives and having dinner all together. My aunt and uncle looked forward to meeting this guy who had taken up residence in my heart. That afternoon, Curtis and my cousin ran around outside playing paintball while Mom and I helped prepare dinner.

The adults were having drinks while sitting on the outside patio when Curtis received a call. He retreated to the guest quarters where he could have some privacy. After some time had passed, I went to check on him. I could hear Curtis objecting frequently under his breath. The conversation was about us—again. The call went on for about an hour when Mom came to find us. I could tell her patience had worn thin. She politely requested that we, or at least I, come outside to join the adults for dinner. She said it was time to visit with relatives we hardly ever had the chance to see.

But Curtis remained on the never-ending phone call, and I wasn't about to leave him. At one point, I heard a distinct sniffle. He hung up as dinner ended.

My aunt and uncle had made arrangements for their family (including their two young daughters) to stay in a nearby hotel, but their son wanted to sleep at the house. Not having the opportunity to get to know Curtis, my aunt was hesitant about my boyfriend staying overnight with my cousin remaining as well. She thought dating teenagers spelled trouble and could possibly set a bad example for her children. Mom said maybe Curtis should go home. Curtis and I looked at each other in a way that said we'd have none of that. We needed to talk, and I needed to know we were okay.

My brother had been camping not long before with his girlfriend, so why couldn't we do the same? Mom, still dumbfounded by the whole missing-dinner ordeal and inconsiderate teenagers, seemed happy to broker a peaceful outcome for everyone attending this small family gathering. So between the cracks of Curtis' fight with his parents and my irritated mother, my boyfriend and I prepared to slip out of the sight of watchful eyes and onto the open road, camping gear and warm clothes piled hastily in the trunk before Mom could change her mind. I couldn't believe she was letting us go. In other circumstances, she would have called the Alexanders, but after what had happened earlier, she was probably avoiding any conversation with them.

As we drove down the highway, the Zac Brown Band serenaded us with one of our favorite songs. The lyrics "Free as we'll ever be" captured the moment and seared it into my memory. The words were so right for us. Our relationship was born before time, before the wind. What were the odds of Curtis coming to Singapore when he did and walking into my English class? Of having so much in common? Of growing so close so fast? Of now living out our dreams in Colorado, my favorite place on earth? If soul mates existed, we were more than that.

I could feel the pain when he hurt and wanted to take it from him, absorbing all of his distress and doubts and making everything okay. But maybe him being okay meant being without me. I thought about this on the way to the campsite and let it soak in. "Just as free, free as we'll ever be." We'd never know freedom like this again apart from schedules, rules, expectations, and boundaries.

We settled in at the campsite and then looked at the stars and contemplated our future. Curtis said he wanted to stay together, but I recognized the same conflict in his voice that I'd heard so long ago on the night of our game of truth or dare when he told me we should just be friends.

Those torn emotions played themselves out over the night. We loved each other. There was no denying that. And that night I felt closer to Curtis than at any other time we'd been together. I thought about the next step. I could possibly hold on to him if we took our relationship to the next level, and I did want him more than ever. As we got caught up in the moment, the ruby stone in my purity ring became snagged in my hair. The event was small, but it was enough for me to regain my senses.

"Curtis, stop. Stop!"

"Angel, what's wrong?"

I sat up and soberly considered the situation. I was almost nineteen and with someone I'd loved for more than two years. What would be the harm in sharing something so special with him? He'd come prepared with protection. And I'd been on birth control for years to help alleviate migraines. Besides, I hadn't had a period for months due to malnourishment. But accidents happen. I doubted my fragile body would even accept a pregnancy. On the other hand, what if I wasn't strong enough to carry the emotional load of having Curtis be my first?

I was already dealing with a disease I couldn't seem to get a handle on. The additional emotional weight of bonding physically with Curtis might put me over the edge—especially if something bad were to happen. I also didn't want him adding a complication to his life right now. What if he needed his freedom but stayed with me out of a sense of duty? I didn't want to make an impulsive decision that could dramatically change us. I was coherent enough to know we both wanted to do more with our lives before dealing with all the imagined complications occupying my mind.

So we cooled down and enjoyed just being together. We talked. We watched the stars. We cuddled. I realized then that real life could be even better than fantasy, and I'd hold this memory close in my heart.

Morning came. Curtis had to get to work. We packed up quickly, and he dropped me at the nearest grocery store where a table outside the entrance provided a convenient pickup point for my mother. We said our good-byes as if we'd see each other soon. Before he turned to leave, I kissed the Maltese cross pendant dangling around his neck. He got in his car and as I watched him drive away, what had existed only hours before rekindled in my memory: the crisp night air, the sound of the water, the smell of earth and his skin, his warm breath whispering my name. It was perfect—almost too perfect.

A faint murmuring from the dark side of my soul begged to be heard, only to be stifled by the weight of true love. Yet, determined to make itself known, it recorded its doubt as a whisper: *Will this be the last time I ever see him?*

College-Bound

As Mom and I passed the Colorado–Utah border, I envisioned my brother on this same route that led him to forty-nine days of wandering the Idaho desert. I found the scene unsettling. Was it my turn to enter the wilderness? Or was I leaving it?

The more I thought about my last few moments with Curtis the more I believed my concerns about seeing him again were nonsense driven by our emotional departure. We had built a strong relationship, and of course his parents would support us visiting each other in college. We'd always found a way back to each other, and now with diminished distance and time zones, I believed we'd regroup after school started, with routine Skype dates and planned visits fueling our anticipation.

I looked forward to visiting his campus, not too far from my father's childhood home. Curtis said he wanted to come out to California too. His school followed a trimester schedule and started after mine.

He could see my new home and then settle into his. Still, apprehension nagged at me as we drove.

The desert required things from those who entered it: meditation, contemplation, self-examination. That bothered me. Right now I craved distraction. Now was not the time to go searching inside myself.

According to a map of Israel my father had shown me, the forty-year wilderness journey of Moses and the Israelites to the Promised Land could have taken only days to complete. They had blamed God for their problems and turned to idol worship. I wondered if I had idols in my own life. Was my love for Curtis forbidden? Did it surpass my love for God? If I were honest, the answer would have to be yes. But was it wrong to love someone that much?

I thought about the times Curtis and I prayed together before meals. I loved that about us. I also thought about a tradition we shared: praying over each other when saying our good-byes. I'd grab his necklace, rub my fingers over the pendant, and pray for God to bless and protect him. He would touch my necklace (one he'd made for me) and return the blessing. Would God now remove the one thing that brought light and sanity into my world? He'd escorted Curtis into my life at the height of my despair. Would He now take him from me?

I opened my purse and pulled out the latest CD from Curtis. He'd written "College Road Trip" across the disc. Music had always bridged the gap between us. It connected us through its rhythm as well as its meaning. CDs or play lists usually accompanied birthday and Christmas presents. My growing collection had phrases and nicknames on each cover. The effort and time Curtis put into song choices affirmed his feelings for me—and for us.

Music also helped fill the void when direct communication seemed inconvenient. One of us might be sleeping when the other needed to talk. Or one of us might be traveling through spotty cell coverage in the desert, hindering chances for a quick call.

I put the CD in the player and listened as a song began—track two, Tim McGraw. It was an upbeat country-music tune about first love, fond memories of two seventeen-year-olds. They had a chance encounter on a plane five years later, and she wondered if he remembered her. He replied that a heart doesn't forget something like that. *What message was Curtis sending now?*

St. George, Utah, ahead. Billboards for Zion National Park dotted the highway, advertising biking and hiking adventures. Daddy would have loved that. Mom and I parked outside Cracker Barrel and skipped across the parking lot. Over dinner, we talked about Vegas—how we would lounge by the Aria pool during the day and stay up late watching the Bellagio fountains at night. Before I realized it, I'd eaten half the order of my French toast. Mom knew exactly what she was doing. I stopped eating, but I had appreciated the diversion.

As we strolled through the Old Country Store, a wooden peg game caught my eye—a possible roommate bonding activity. Mom paid the bill (including the peg game) then put her arm tightly around my waist and escorted me out of the double swinging doors. A beautiful sunset awaited us.

"Aren't the colors beautiful?" my mother asked, pointing toward the horizon above some distant mountains.

The deep pinks and purples reminded me of evening family walks in Texas.

Then she added, "There's a Target nearby. Let's get some snacks for the room."

My pulse accelerated. I turned my head away from her in an effort to erase what she'd said. Guilt always sets in soon after a meal. Thinking about food was the last thing I wanted right then. A courtroom drama began playing out in my head, and the syrupy sweetness lingering in my mouth had been called as a last-minute witness to testify against me. My monster appeared front and center ready to prosecute.

You shouldn't have eaten that, it reprimanded me. *You'll be bloated in the morning. And you want to lie out by the pool in a bikini? You know carbs aren't good for you, and your mother made you eat them. She tricked you, actually, by engaging you in conversation. How could you give in like that?*

Whenever guilt came accusing, my logical side would counter with the fact that a body runs on energy and that energy comes from carbs. But the monster inside would harness the science and further expand the logic by advising, *Yes, but it's late and your body is ready to shut down and will store the carbs and turn them into fat.* My monster always had a comeback. And that night my emotional side was in overdrive, contemplating loss and change in my transitioning life. I didn't say anything to Mom but dutifully coerced my feet to follow her into the store, the big red Target bull's-eye watching my every move.

Taking a basket, Mom went off in search of dried fruit and Luna bars. I found myself in a haze as I struggled with the guilt but the confusion quickly cleared as I realized I didn't have much time. If Mom found me with my basket empty, we'd search together for snacks, and that meant I wouldn't be able to think on my own.

I bolted toward the back of the store, far from the candy aisle. Mom would certainly check out some sweets before searching for me. I walked quickly, reasoning that the speed of my gait would influence my brain to come up with something. *Come on. Come on. Come … on!*

The sound of a cooing baby caught my attention. I watched as he passed, his mother smiling as the little boy reached into an open package and pulled out something that looked like purple Cheerios. *Baby food! That's it! There's my answer!*

Without further thought, I started looking for the baby food aisle. Where was it? Aware my time was ticking away, I almost ran through the store.

Found it! Now what was that kid eating? Echoes of the cooing baby drove me. I wanted that snack! *There it is.* I took a deep breath and looked up and down the aisle. There was no one around.

Gerber Graduates Yogurt Melts. Says they're for toddlers. Sounded safe but I had to be sure. Toddlers meant growing babies. I did not want to grow. Better check the nutritional content, after all. Anything under one hundred calories would be a go. I painstakingly turned the package around and scanned the back label.

"Corinne!"

My mother's voice and stunned expression startled me. I knew I looked guilty. She'd caught me in the act.

"Honey?"

Her voice sounded soft and caring. I could only stare at her, eyes wide, no response. A long pause followed. Mom stood there searching my countenance. I looked down and noticed her holding a large bag of gummy Swedish Fish, a recent addition to her candy addiction, thanks to Curtis.

Finally, I could tell it registered with her—the aisle I was in, the baby food in my hand. She started to cry and laugh at the same time. So did I.

"Do you want those?"

I think she was happy I'd selected anything at all. "No?"

She approached, dropped the candy bag, and hugged me tight.

"You're okay. It's okay. You'll be fine. We'll get to L.A. and find some help. In-house treatment or start school—it doesn't matter. It doesn't matter, sweetheart. Dad and I support you. Whatever you need. Let's just get you well."

I took in my mother's smell and breathed deeply. Coco Chanel, her favorite. She cradled me like a baby—gently swaying back and forth—and for a full minute, I experienced complete rest. It was I who initiated the next move. Feeling, and receiving, the unconditional love and acceptance in that moment, I placed the toddler snack back on the shelf and privately vowed not to venture into the baby aisle again until I had a child of my own.

A few days later when I set foot on to Chapman's Southern California campus, I knew I was home. I could see myself thriving there. Sunshine and blue skies. Small campus. Greek life. Service clubs. A beautiful interfaith chapel with stained-glass windows. Old Towne City of Orange down the street, littered with tearooms, modern retail, an old soda fountain and diner, Starbucks, and throwback '50s-style gift shops. Newport Beach was maybe a twenty-minute drive.

But would anyone here understand me? How could anyone identify with what I was going through? The me before anorexia would have looked down on people who had this illness, because I'd once believed it was their choice. I thought people with eating disorders woke up one day and said to themselves, *I look fat, so I'll just stop eating until I'm thin.*

Looking back, I no longer judged those girls who struggled with an illness I knew nothing about. Maybe Judgment had dragged me off of her throne to join the girls I'd pitied. How naïve I'd been. They'd probably been oppressed by the same obsessive thoughts now plaguing me. I wondered what they'd called the voice or voices that sometimes advised, sometimes harassed, sometimes screamed. ED (eating disorder)? Monster? Something else?

Maybe we were we all striving for perfection: perfect grades, perfect image, perfect bodies—riddled by guilt when we didn't measure up to the expectations implanted in our brains. I came to see the girls I'd once belittled now as sisters sharing the same destructive cycle—eat, guilt, starve.

I wondered how I'd make it at Chapman—an epicenter of beach bikinis and high achievers. I wanted college, though—the experience, the learning, the degree—maybe even more than my consuming desire to be thin. *Maybe I could have both.* I decided I had to stay in control and make this work. I resolved to be a functioning anorexic; no one would know. I wouldn't come out of the closet. I'd find a way to balance the eating disorder so I could go to school and keep my parents happy.

I promised my parents I would see a therapist as well as a nutritionist each week as an alternative to in-house treatment. Mom and Dad would regularly check in to make sure I kept my end of the bargain. I had no problem with that plan. Research and communication were my strong suits. Assuring and persuading people, after all, were among my specialties. I'd say the right words and make even the experts believe I wasn't sick.

Chapman provided psychological counseling without additional charge; the services came with tuition. My therapist, Linda, scheduled our meetings for Wednesdays at three. The nutritionist, although not affiliated with the school, came highly recommended. Mom reassured me that the two of them, Susan and Linda, would work together to provide me the best of care. Susan's office was minutes from campus. I'd see her each Monday at five with a follow-up phone session Thursday afternoons.

I soon came to dread Mondays. I despised my nutritionist, not because she was unkind, but because she made me question everything I believed about my body. She said I was dangerously thin, but I could still see unwanted fat around my belly, my abdomen appearing swollen and distended. It wasn't as my parents said it would be. Susan was not my ally. She was my worst enemy, and I resented her for trying to distort my way of thinking. The only thing that kept me going to our sessions was Chapman—the place I now called home and had come to love. I didn't want to risk my parents pulling me out of school.

Woven Like Licorice

"Four years that last a lifetime. Recruitment 2011." Posters with Greek letters and invitations offering sisterhood lined the halls of Chapman's Student Union. The idea of having a sister or sisters around the same age both troubled and intrigued me. I'd always shied away from cliques. The idea of girls gathering to gossip or judge each other on fashion sense didn't appeal to me.

By this time I'd seen plenty of TV shows and movies portraying college life. It looked to me as though sororities offered girls the opportunity to compete, look good, and stay thin—a feeding frenzy for my monster. But the vibe around campus seemed fun and friendly, and the girls weren't all thin. I'd observed a wide range of looks, body styles, and fashion. The sorority girls at Chapman seemed welcoming and sweet. I found each one of them gorgeous, inside and out.

Sophe said she was going to the information meeting. I thought maybe I should go, too.

Sophe and I met at a gathering for new students during the summer in Colorado. She grew up in Vail, the closest thing to home I'd ever known, so we met for lunch in Vail Village and e-mailed several times before check-in day on campus. We ended up moving into the same dorm and bought Disneyland passes along with the idea that the happiest place on earth would provide the answer to any bad day.

I thought about the girls I'd seen around campus, and I thought about Sophe. If my experiences so far represented college life, then joining a sorority might not be that bad. At least I'd have the option to socialize. I'd also have a built-in support network—an important consideration, seeing that my family lived so far away. Maybe these girls could help fill the void. Maybe there'd be a place for me in going Greek.

"Okay, girls, it's time to pump up on some sugar!" A tall, stunning African American girl stood before me, twirling red licorice. She smiled as she held out a strand of edible rope. I bit my lip and quickly but kindly turned down her offer. I couldn't be tempted.

The girl introduced herself as a rho gamma, one of the "mothers" of recruitment, selected to take care of the girls going through rush. Sororities offered girls an opportunity to be a part of something bigger, to bond with an instant sisterhood, woven together in purpose and friendship. Woven like the licorice held by the beautiful girl.

Excited about rush.

What was advertised as an exhilarating experience turned out to be a difficult and tiring ritual. As part of the process, girls paraded through sorority meet and greets while perched upon high heels hour after blister-burning hour. Some even dressed in their finest attire, hair flawlessly curled or straightened, masking tired faces with Laura Mercier and toting the latest Chanel bags.

My schedule became packed from Friday to Sunday. On Friday I visited all of the chapters and interviewed with more than thirty girls. For someone on a highly restricted diet, to be "on" for hours at a time made it extremely difficult to function. The lack of nutrition caused my body to respond in sluggish rebellion. My vision became impaired. My mouth dried up. Impressions of reality couldn't reach my brain fast enough, leaving my mind muddled. I had to work particularly hard to make sense of my surroundings. Sophe could tell something was wrong and tried to help. I told her about my illness but assured her I had a handle on it.

At one point I nearly fainted. Blackness crept in from my peripheral vision. The blood rushed from my head, leaving me pale and breathless. Without thinking, I reached out and clutched the arm next to mine to help ground my wobbling knees. I shut my eyes and thought, *You can do this.*

Two deep breaths later, I found my bearings, determination alone giving me a second wind. Locking my knees, I straightened my posture and pried open my eyes.

"Are you okay?" a soft whisper came from my right.

Our rho gamma. I looked down and realized I had her arm in a death grip.

"Oh my gosh. I am so sorry!"

I cupped my hand over my mouth, flustered at my faux pas. I'd inflicted pain on the kind girl looking after me.

"It's okay, honey, but are you all right?"

Her gaze expressed concerned.

"Yeah … yeah, I'm fine. It's been a long day."

I scanned the floor, avoiding her eyes. I wasn't a good liar.

"You know if you need anything, I'm here," she said softly. "Okay?"

I nodded, and she embraced me. I couldn't help but feel guilty.

I reflected on what the licorice-twirling girl had said to me. "You know if you need anything, I'm here." She'd looked so sincere and sounded so gentle. There was an authenticity about her that made me think sorority life offered exactly what the poster indicated. Maybe the friendships made here *could* last a lifetime.

That thought then made me nervous. A lifetime. Friends, sisters—for life. I'd gone into rush with the idea of exploring Greek life and the possibility of sisterhood. I hadn't considered how hard it would be to choose between the sororities. Three chapters captured my attention, but each of them represented a different personality, different service opportunities, different girls. What if I chose the wrong one? What if my top pick didn't want me? Could I join and keep my eating disorder a secret?

All the questions kept me up Saturday night as I wondered about the perfect fit. My tendency to spin thoughts into obsession meant I didn't sleep at all. Anorexic prophesying permeated my mind, telling me the more people I had around me—and in my business—the harder it would be to keep my secret. Sooner or later, I'd be found out. But I also saw one of my roommates struggling and becoming isolated. She'd had other commitments during orientation and had missed out on many of the social activities. She didn't know many people and spent a lot of time alone.

I decided I had to be as social as possible and get to know as many people as I could. My need for belonging overruled my fear of being found out. I'd be exhausted with the schedule, but I was willing to pay that price for friendship.

After the long and tiring journey through recruitment, I chose my family and it chose me. I ran out along with the other recruits. Sophe and I ran together to officially join the girls of Gamma Phi Beta. Crescent moon. Pink carnation. Sisters for life. Gratitude welled up inside me. I'd managed to keep a positive attitude and a smile on my face, which gave me the will to push forward and find the sorority that fit me best.

All of us gathered on the steps of Memorial Hall and posed for a group photo. My world became smaller, more intimate. I found it an honor to say I'd become a member of Gamma Phi. The sorority gave me new purpose, and for the first time in a long time, I felt like I belonged.

Black and White

Friday, September 16. A jam-packed morning of newbie meetings and shell shock. It had been an exciting week. I'd received a bid from Gamma Phi, accepted it as my first choice, and was now learning what it meant to be a pledge. Gamma Phi's catchphrase, "To the moon and back," had been one of the sign-offs Curtis and I used when we ended a chat session. Now I'd use that same phrase with my sisters.

I couldn't wait to tell Curtis about all that had happened, but the long rush sessions and first meetings left me exhausted, and I hadn't eaten much of anything. Unnerved by my lack of energy, I determined to talk with my boyfriend before attending to my other needs.

Curtis and I had a call scheduled at 1 p.m. I'd go to the cafeteria after that. I waited. And waited. I kept checking the time on my computer screen. One hour later and still no call. *Where is he, and why so late?* Why was I waiting? I'd never done this before. There were times in the past when Curtis had missed a Skype session, and when he had, I'd given him ten minutes then redirected my thoughts and activities elsewhere. We'd even discussed the issue; he'd improved his punctuality.

I needed sleep and food and couldn't get either. I kept waiting. My mind raced. I presumed the lack of nourishment in my system exaggerated my emotions, but I couldn't distance myself from the rush of doubt surging through my bloodstream. Questions filled my head then a fleeting thought shot across the bow of my brain. *Could I, a communications major, end up with someone who struggled in that area?*

What am I thinking? I must be exhausted. None of my processing made sense or mattered. I loved Curtis, and besides, every relationship encounters tough times. I'd do whatever it took to hold on to what we had. So I ignored the warning blip on my radar screen, dismissing it as quickly as it had appeared. We'd always made our relationship work before, and that was when I was half a world away. We were on the same side of the planet now; Chicago only a couple of hours away by plane. This time would be no different. We'd be fine.

He finally called.

"I'm so sorry, angel. I forgot my phone on my bed."

He paused. "Time got away from me with all the meetings. You okay?"

"Curtis, I've been waiting here. We were supposed to talk at 1 p.m."

I sounded frantic. He waited a second before answering.

"Communication's a problem for me—I know." He paused again and lowered his voice.

"Corinne, I'm just not sure—about anything."

He let that sink in.

"I'm so busy right now with the beginning of school, and I keep letting you down," he said.

I didn't pause or think, but immediately solved his quandary for him.

"I'm gonna make this easy for you, Curtis. We need space. I'll give you some time to figure out what you want."

I spoke so quickly that I wasn't completely sure of what I'd said. All I knew was that I had to get off the phone. My mind wasn't working well and I couldn't make sense of anything either one of us was saying.

"Two weeks. Let's give it two weeks. I have to go," I said.

"Okay, Corinne."

"Bye, Curtis."

We signed off cordially enough. I changed my Facebook status, taking off anything to do with my relationship, and as I pressed the enter key a chill ran through my body. I sat still for a moment and thought about what just happened, and as I processed the call, an emotional riptide pulled Curtis out of my reach—and trailing behind him, the remnants of my appetite.

I lay down on my bed. Two weeks. What would Curtis choose? I was all in. Was he? I wondered if he'd miss me. Miss us. And if he did miss us, would his feelings override the practical thoughts *too young* and *what if*? Although his academic interests focused on engineering, Curtis had a creative and emotional side as well. Which side would prevail? I thought I caught a glimpse of a storm cloud on the horizon of our fairy tale's powder-blue skies.

Either way I prayed for his happiness and for God to care for and watch over him. I decided to write his parents to let them know what had happened. Mr. Alexander later responded with an appropriate "We think the world of you" and bromides about college life—all too vague and distant to recall.

After sending the e-mail, I felt sick. I had to get out of my dorm, away from what represented the stifling confines of indecision. *I can't breathe. I need fresh air.* I started my car, and the music began where it left off. "Don't turn your back on what you think you know. You never know." The song—"You Are My Kind" by Santana—played from the CD Curtis had made for me before the road trip from Denver to Los Angeles. The lyrics engulfed the car. *That's the last thing I need to hear.* Feverishly tapping the eject button, I couldn't stop the unrequested song fast enough before a vision of us flashed before my eyes. The interrupted disc finally peeked out from my CD player. I threw it onto the back seat. At that moment, I wanted everything having to do with Curtis thrown behind me.

Another Monday meeting with Susan. Several weeks had passed and I still couldn't trust her because I didn't believe all her scientific blather about my body. I did pay attention to her, though. She exuded success: striking yet approachable, knowledgeable in her field, blond, tall, strong, and lean. I sat in the waiting room before my appointments and observed the patients who left her office.

One lady walked with a cane. She was overweight. I watched as, over several sessions, her weight decreased. One day the office door opened and as the lady exited, I noticed she no longer required assistance. She told Susan that she was beginning to feel better. She walked by me with a quicker gait. I considered her statement and agreed—losing did feel good.

I'd enter Susan's chambers for each appointment, take a seat, and lie about the things I ate. Most of the time, my efforts would focus on the clock, counting down the seconds until our session ended. I couldn't stand it. Tick. Tick. Tick. Blah. Blah. Blah.

"Your body has to learn to trust you again. And yes, your stomach will respond at first by storing fat around your midsection in order to protect your organs. But over time, Corinne, the weight will redistribute once your body knows it won't be thrown into starvation mode again."

No way I'd agree to that. I already had enough fat around my midsection—fat I was trying to remove. I'd arrive at each appointment early so I could think about the lies I'd tell. I had never lied before, not like this. I actually prided myself on honesty. Now I plotted and schemed and had to remember which lies I'd told and when so Susan would believe me. (I hoped she believed me.)

Did she know? She'd call my name and I'd sit down in the same spot and offer the disinformation I'd made up moments before. Then I'd leave, feeling the same way as when I'd entered—with a little added guilt about lying.

One day something changed as our session ended. As usual I couldn't wait to leave. I had to get to a sorority meeting and considered this a waste of time. My foot bounced up and down the final five minutes, keeping time with the ticking in my mind.

Finally, done.

Feeling like a grade-school kid at the three o'clock bell, I opened the door and took off for my Chapman playground. But as I looked up, I saw something that caught me off guard. A girl about my age sat waiting in the chair next to the interrogation room I'd just escaped. As I walked past her, we made eye contact. She was gorgeous. We looked at each other like we were staring into some sort of mirror—one that held similar secrets behind its thin veneer.

Her hair was blond and long like mine. She had bright blue eyes. Had I seen her before at some Greek event? She looked familiar. She smiled, so I returned the gesture then made a beeline for the door. I should have said something, but the situation stunned me. I'd never before seen a girl my age there. All I could do was hope and pray I'd never see her again. She was the only one—outside of my family and a few close friends—who knew about my clandestine meetings on Chapman Avenue.

Three days before Curtis and I were scheduled to talk again, I received a text: "Corinne, no matter what happens, I'm sure we want to be in each other's lives because of how much we mean to each other."

My pulse soared as my soul screamed betrayal.

I'd always seen the world in black and white. There was no gray. Actions were either good or bad. You won or you lost. You made an A or you didn't. People loved you or they left you. Anorexia takes that trait and holds a magnifier over it, making any event or conversation a big deal. The one sentence Curtis wrote sounded distant. Definitely black.

Determined and focused, my feet took command of my body, stepping in military fashion to gather my friends in the foxhole for the final stand. This would happen on my turf and on my time. Armed with the support of my allies, I made the call.

"Hi, angel!" He sounded like nothing was wrong.

"Curtis, we need to talk," I said.

He asked if he could call me right back and said he loved me. I didn't say it back.

The phone rang. My weapons were raised, safeties off. We volleyed words and phrases—including many I can't remember—in a tone I didn't recognize as "us." The discussion wasn't heated, but definitely guarded.

"Our relationship doesn't have to be defined by a title," Curtis said, taking a position I deemed unfamiliar.

Gray. That went against everything I'd ever known. Could I possibly accept gray? My heart started to give in to his rationale. Then I looked at my friends, the reinforcements I needed. Their eyes said it all.

Be strong, Corinne.

Curtis continued, "Corinne, first semester is like navigating white water rapids and …"

And there they were—the exact words Curtis' dad had written me in his e-mail—those empty platitudes that now wounded my trusting and tender heart. I tried to pinpoint the moment I had lost my worth in Curtis' mind. I tuned back into the conversation.

"I don't want contacting you to be an obligation," he said.

Who is this? Now I'm in the same sentence with the word "obligation"? I was no longer a priority. *Where is my Curtis, the one who said, "You're my family now, Corinne"?* This had to be some sort of delusion or nightmare. Surely I'd wake up and realize we were fine.

"Corinne, I don't want to hurt you anymore."

No, this was not my imagination.

But this did hurt. Giving up hurt. Leaving me hurt. Time slowed to a comatose pace as I tried to process his theory on relationships, but it didn't compute with anything I rendered as truth.

My hands tingled. I held up the right one for inspection and recognized the telltale loss of vision. I figured I had about five minutes before the hammering on my brain began. I'd welcome the distraction. At least it would bring on a pain I could name. I couldn't bear the script Curtis had written for the end of us.

I had to go.

My friends hovered close, resting their hands on my thigh and stroking my back, giving me the courage I needed to respond.

"Curtis, I wish the best for you, and I hope someday you'll find a girl worth fighting for."

I hung up and hyperventilated, readying myself for the mental and physical onslaught. Time to surrender to my premonitions about this moment—and to the migraine worming its way through my head.

Fallout

I woke up, startled. Darkness filled my room. Quiet filled it too. Even my monster was silent. My roommate slept soundly. The clock read 3:04 a.m. Someone had buried me alive and had forgotten to leave in my casket the string attached to the bell above my grave. It didn't matter, though. Even if there were a way to sound an alarm, who would come dig me out of this hole?

A far-off echo ripped through my mind. "I'll always be here for you, angel." That was no longer the case. And although Mom had just been here, my parents lived on the other side of the planet. What could they do? I thought of my sorority sisters, especially Sophe. I was growing closer to them and loved being a Gamma Phi, but I didn't feel enough of a bond to trouble someone with a middle-of-the-night call for help.

My head still pounded with a strong ache, but at least it wasn't the hammering of a migraine. What had happened? Everything had shifted so fast. I was single.

One conversation had changed my whole world. I understood Curtis' reasoning. It made sense. I'd heard the first semester of college led to breakups for many high school holdouts. But most of those couples had a lot of fights, intermittently getting back together, only to finally end with animosity. I didn't want that—would not have that—for us. The break would be clean and swift. We would move on. Black and white. It happens.

But not to us. We were different, weren't we? I wondered if one person in every breakup believed that. Why couldn't we have broken up when I was ready? Right after prom. *We discussed this.*

I started to grieve in my own mechanical, sadistic way. After all, I'd been waiting, almost with anticipation, for this day. But a part of me still ached for Curtis to make that late-night call, the one where we'd toss aside inhibitions and let feelings fly, where he'd tell me everything I wanted to hear and fight the monster in my mind—and our parents—just to be with me.

I did receive a call that night. I let it go to voicemail and retrieved it upon waking. What I wanted would never happen; Curtis had called to say there had been a misunderstanding—that he'd thought about ending our relationship during the summer. I would have preferred that.

And so it was the end of our story—a fairy tale I'd made up in my mind of a princess who'd lived in a faraway land and who was loved by an OsoPrinceCreeper.

The mid-autumn festival falls on the eighth month of the lunar calendar, a time of celebration back in Asia. My parents would be out watching children carrying colorful battery-operated lanterns that emitted catchy tunes and blinking lights, enjoying a full moon, fireworks, and deferred bedtimes. During this season family, friends, and coworkers exchange circular mooncakes of various flavors and meanings. The cakes carry Chinese symbols of love and harmony or representations of the seasonal tale of Chang E, who lived on the moon with her pet rabbit. Traditional pastries filled with lotus seed, red-bean paste and nuts, or salted duck eggs are cut into small wedges and served with Chinese tea. A mooncake with a double yolk is the most desirable, representing double happiness.

I wasn't feeling that way.

The story of Chang E and her skilled archer, Houyi, has many variations. In my favorite plot, the princess accidentally takes an immortality pill and floats off toward the moon, leaving her hero bound to the earth and yearning to shoot her down to keep her from drifting farther away. He never fires his arrow, however, for he cannot bear the thought of hurting her.

I was now the princess, the full moon drawing me to it like Chang E floating to the heavens. I'd ingested a poison that separated me forever from the one I loved. Standing between two worlds parting beneath his feet, my hero found himself restrained by the rational world, holding his bow while I accelerated toward the moon with my pet rabbit. There would be no going back.

I spent the following day curled up on my bed. I settled in for what I knew best: abandonment. I reached for my sweatshirt—his sweatshirt—that I'd worn so long. His smell now lingered too close for comfort. Holding my breath, I quickly packed his remains away in a temporary cardboard casket in the holding area beneath my dorm room bed. I grabbed a substitute fleece, trying to stave off the emotional chill in the air. The only remnant of my first love would now exist in uninvited dreams that eased the pain of my nightmarish days. Sleep came easily.

Turquoise organza flows over strappy heels. My knees are bent, submitting to a techno beat. I'm singing, "And I owe it all to you." I jump up, pointing my fingers to the ceiling, and yell, "I've had the time of my li-i-ife, and I've never felt this way before." Lights flash. Party dresses and tuxes tumble around the room in a kaleidoscope of color. I'm sweating. So is he. The pins holding my bun are coming loose; I can feel my hair unraveling. He's behind me, touching me, keeping my rhythm. I love it when we dance. I turn around to steal a kiss, and as I do, my wrist corsage snags on the button of his shirt and comes untied. I bend down to retrieve it and notice the floor littered with purple prom tickets. I reach down to pick up the now-dried flowers and stand to find an empty room, lights on. I'm all alone.

"Corinne, wake up. You okay?" My roommate seemed concerned. "You screamed."

"Did I say anything?"

"No, just a brief scream. You okay?"

"Yeah, yeah. I'm fine. I'll be fine. What time is it?"

"Ten after six."

"I'm so sorry. Go back to sleep. I'm going for a run."

One thing about anorexia: it's consistent and dependable. When something bad happens, it offers the same answer time and time again. Exercise and don't eat.

With breakups there's always fallout. Keepsakes are sorted into the following piles: memory box, return to sender, and trash. Friends are divided into his and hers, and few remain in the both category. Respective family members opt out and immediately default into the shallow recesses of Christmas-card form letters and belated birthday wishes.

But breakups also bring with them unforeseen consequences. I neatly folded the post-prom T-shirt that I'd never wear again and thought of the twins, Curtis' sisters. A few weeks ago I'd stopped by the Alexander home to drop off two necklaces my dad purchased for them at the Pearl Market while he was in Beijing on a business trip—gifts for their eleventh birthday.

I loved those girls. I imagined them as the little sisters I'd begged my mom to have. They were easy to be with, and I always looked forward to spending time with them whether we were on the Jump Street trampolines, playing around the house, making spider pretzels for Halloween, or walking the dogs. Anything was fine with me as long as we were all together.

Now what? What was I supposed to do about them? Call them and say, "I'm sorry it didn't work out with your brother and me, but …"? But what? I didn't want to risk getting upset while talking with them. And my illness added to my resolve in remaining silent on the matter. The girls must have noticed my decreasing frame toward the end of summer. We'd gone bowling one afternoon, and I couldn't keep my size 00 pants up. I wasn't about to expose them to more of this disease. I knew their parents would tell them something that sounded reasonable.

Two days passed. Two days since my life changed in a way I hadn't seen coming. I didn't want to eat. I didn't want to see anyone. I just wanted to sleep, and so I did, taking my chances in a world where nightmares seemed better than what I had to face when awake.

When I woke up I thought I'd missed a call from Curtis. I thought we were okay. I stretched my arms and smiled.

Then I remembered. My smile faded. My throat constricted. My body tingled, and a cold shiver ran up my arms. Too much. All of it—way too much. Sorting out memories and packing up my past had tipped me over the edge.

Emptiness filled me. I couldn't function anymore. I couldn't think about life—the future, the present. The heaviness of it made me tired—tired of thinking, talking, breathing. I was done trying to be happy, trying to act successful and energetic, trying to matter. I began to welcome the idea of melting away into a state of nothingness where the constant fight to live the fantasy of a fulfilled life would finally come to an end. No more pain. No more worry. No more pressure.

I could let go, surrender, and say I'd given life my best shot. It seemed easier to die than continue living under the pressure. I'd caused my parents worry for too long. The stress of grades and sorority and breathing shut me down to the point of madness, and I found no answer, not even through prayer.

God had always been a big part of my life. By the age of eight years old, my pastor in Rockwall, Texas, baptized me after I kept telling Mom and Dad I was ready. I believed. And I loved my Jesus. I said my prayers each night before bed and thanked Him for all the blessings in my life. My parents said tough times would come, and that when they did, God would always provide comfort and a way of escape.

Not true. Not now. I prayed for healing. I read my Bible. I searched the Psalms for comfort. No matter what I did, though, I didn't feel Him, didn't hear Him, didn't sense His power or protection in my life.

I thought if God was out there watching, maybe He would forgive me and welcome me home to an eternity where I wouldn't hurt anymore. Thinking about death calmed me. A strange peace came with the idea of it. I told God if He didn't give me some sign of His presence, I'd find a way to end my pain.

Soon after I finished my pseudo prayer, there came a knock on my door.

Forcing my body out of bed, I lumbered to the door, opened it, and realized how much effort that simple task had taken. It was Sophe.

"Hi. You okay?" she asked.

I turned to leave her at the opening, but she trailed right behind me.

"Hi. I'm okay," I said, walking back to my bed and falling into the comfortable fetal position. "Why are you here?"

"You missed the meeting. Didn't you get my texts?" she asked.

"No. My phone must have been on silent. I let Maddy know I wasn't coming. I haven't been feeling well."

"I just felt like I should come down here and check on you. Have you slept all day?"

I looked up for a brief moment, wondering if God was being humorous or caring, but either way the question was enough to jar my apathy, for the moment anyway.

"I studied some. I'm good."

Not really. And Sophe knew.

"Come on. Let's go to the caf. You need to eat." She sat on the side of my bed and gently touched my leg. "I'll wait right here until you're ready."

There was no getting out of this. Sophe could be stubborn and convincing. I grumbled, but soaked up the love and attention she showered on me. I threw on a T-shirt and sweatpants, put my hair up in a bun, and followed her out the door, grabbing my sweatshirt on the way.

We found an open table. I put my sweatshirt on a chair to hold my place. Then we took off in different directions. I headed for the salad bar.

Sophe came back to the table to find me playing with a few peas on my plate.

"Corinne, look at me."

I ignored her. I didn't want to talk.

"Corinne, please. Please get something to eat," she implored.

I guessed she wasn't thrilled with my food choice.

I looked up at her, a tear clouding my vision. I wanted to make her feel good, so I smiled.

"You're right," I said. "I'll go get something more."

My mouth numbed at the thought of food. I wiped away the tear with the back of my hand, wishing it were that easy to shed my despair. Slowly, I eased my chair from the table, hoping to God someone would pull the fire alarm as a prank so I could escape.

I passed familiar faces, keeping my head down, praying no one would stop me for a chat. I stood in line. My stomach turned. I wanted to be alone, to crawl up into a little ball and slowly disappear.

I had never experienced such loss. My heart was ripping apart, and I could feel every tear. Open heart surgery without anesthesia. Actually, it seemed more like an autopsy performed on a walking corpse. I was dead, but revived repeatedly to experience the torment of a cold scalpel, slicing and separating muscle tissue. The findings would be placed in a file labeled "Broken heart." I could have saved them the effort and told them myself, but I lacked the energy to care.

Memories haunted me as I realized I'd never again experience the warmth and touch of someone who'd been my everything.

I placed my hands on my head, pressing hard against my skull in an attempt to mute the remembrances and relieve the emotional pressure. Another migraine coming on.

"Corinne?"

I jumped at the sound of my name and turned to find a beautiful pale-skinned blonde.

"It's Lindsey. Are you okay?" Her high-pitched voice came across as soft and full of concern.

I couldn't help it. The faucet opened full force, and I shook my head back and forth, not believing my lack of self-control. Without a word, she embraced me. *So this is sisterhood.* I'd met Lindsey during recruitment, and although our meeting had been brief, my intuition noted her kindness. I pulled away from her grasp, embarrassment reprimanding me for my outburst.

"I'm sorry. My boyfriend."

I paused, trying to catch my breath, realizing that term no longer applied to Curtis.

"My boyfriend and I just broke up," I announced.

A third, unfamiliar voice entered the conversation. It belonged to a girl with little-mermaid red hair and blue eyes.

"Oh honey, no, don't be sorry," said the redhead.

She embraced me. I recognized her as another member of Gamma Phi.

"Honey, you're better off without him. We're here for you," she continued.

These girls were seeing me at my worst and loving me anyway. I had to at least try to make this sorority thing work.

But how? If I wasn't careful, I could lose Chapman and my sorority. I appealed to my illness. Maybe we could strike a deal: I could at least attend classes and some sorority events, and it could have control over everything else. My monster emerged from its silence and agreed.

Over the next several days, I quickly learned another way to anesthetize the pain and to avoid the questions and the knocks on my door. Busyness. I went to the store and bought boxes of Malt-O-Meal with individual packets. I'd wake up early, prepare breakfast in my dorm room, and determine to make the energy last all day. My first priority in the morning steered me to the gym for a hard workout. Then I could focus on school. Adrenaline surges from periodic flashbacks helped feed my monster, who would then counsel me to focus my thoughts elsewhere. If I felt weak, my monster gave me permission to grab an apple from the Student Union.

My face appeared brave as I feigned confidence. I aimed to act as every other college girl. I went out, had fun, and experimented. No one would suspect that pain consumed me. As long as I didn't have to think on my own, I could cope. A regimented schedule and anorexia's instructions would get me through the day.

But while I made a lot of friends during this time, loneliness pervaded my spirit. My parents were thousands of miles away, my ex-boyfriend left me without a confidant, and God's presence seemed sporadic at best.

Prayers went unanswered; silent cries for help, unnoticed. The torturous voice of anorexia was my only counsel, and I listened, for being thin still brought me quite a lot of attention.

Birthday Bashed

Mom landed at LAX on October 8 and took a cab to Orange. She tried to hide her concern, but my mother had never been a good liar. I expected what I saw on her face. My weight had plummeted to 88.2 pounds. The skin between my arm and my would-be pectoral muscle looked like it belonged to that of an elderly person. It lacked elasticity and contained minimal tissue.

She hugged me tight. It hurt. My bones, muscles, and emotions had all deteriorated. After collecting herself, Mom offered a pleasant hello to my roommate and asked what Miss Manners would find proper for the occasion. She then turned to me.

"Corinne, would you like to stay with me this evening?" she asked.

I couldn't grab my laptop and lanyard fast enough. We scampered out of the dorm and through the parking structure like prisoners on the loose, making no attempt to contain our excitement. Mom eased into the driver's seat of my little blue sports car, injected Evanescence into the CD player, put the top down, and headed for the Hyatt in Newport Beach.

"Hello, Mrs. Weber," said the hotel attendant. "Good to see you again."

We checked in then made our way to the room where wine, cheese, fresh fruit, and a welcome card greeted us.

I needed Mom and longed for her to tell me I was going to be okay. She directed me to eat. I ate. She told me to take a warm shower. Her instructions were soothing. I relaxed with Mom in charge. The anorexic thoughts quieted, their reprimands stifled by my mother's reassurances.

We crawled into bed and held each other. It took Mom a while to get comfortable. My jagged shoulder blades and spear-like ribs didn't fit into their regular cuddle spots. Mom would have to adjust to a new normal.

After a week of having my mother in town, I was able to regroup a little. That following Saturday morning, I woke up with my mother sleeping soundly behind me. I'd slept well too. I turned slowly to look at the clock; the surprise of waking up later than expected catapulted me out of bed. I never slept this late.

"Mom! It's 11:15. Banner and chant starts in forty-five minutes. I can't be late!"

Banner and chant, a Greek event ending a week of friendly competition and community-building among

Chapman's fraternities and sororities, consists of a three-minute themed dance or cheer performed by each chapter. This year's theme: animation generation.

We quickly found our bearings, threw on some clothes and headed for school—a thirty-minute trek from the Hyatt on a good day.

"Hey, we got here with five minutes to spare." Mom stopped at a food cart. "Can you smell the cinnamon?"

She was hungry. A sign above the bagel-lined basket read, "Bagel Me! Best bagels on Earth."

"Corinne, it's your birthday. Calories don't count on your birthday. And besides, you didn't have breakfast."

I peered into the cart at the warm decadence. I breathed in scents of savory and sweet. Cheese, garlic, blueberry, cinnamon. What I would give to have one of each.

"Maybe later. Come on. It's about to start, and I wanna try to get a good seat," I said.

We found two seats close to the stage. Then, out of nowhere, someone hugged me—the red-haired Ariel girl from the cafeteria who'd seen me bawling. She held a brown paper bag and a string attached to a helium balloon. She sat down next to me.

"Here. These are for you. I knew today was your birthday and I wanted it to start off special."

The paper bag now rested on my lap while my right hand clenched the balloon. Her energy startled me.

Mom looked pleased. She seemed happy with my choice of sorority. The girl revealed her name, introducing herself to my mother. Delaney. I'd remember her now.

"Mrs. Weber, Corinne's such a great addition to Gamma Phi. We love her already."

"She seems to feel at home here. This group of girls fits her."

"Yes, ma'am." Delaney pointed to the bag. "I should have bought two, but I think it's big enough to share. I have to go, but Corinne, meet over there as soon as chant is over. We'll take a group photo."

Delaney pointed to the far-right side of the seating area. I hugged the girl who was already watching over me.

"Thank you! Thank you so much! I cannot tell you how much this means to me!"

"No thanks needed. Just know you've got a sister who loves you."

She smiled and turned to leave.

"Oh, and by the way, take off that sweatshirt! It's eighty-seven degrees out here!"

I nodded and watched her fade into the crowd. Delaney clearly had no idea I was sick.

"Corinne, open it!"

Mom beamed at the offering. I opened the bag to find a huge moist muffin top with a coarse sugar crust and bulging whole blueberries. Excitement and anxiety competed for the moment. Excitement was definitely ahead. I quickly closed the bag, teasing my mother.

"It's mine!" I said.

"What? She said it was big enough to share. Let me see!" I know my mom; she'd do anything for something sweet.

"No," I countered. During our playful game of tug-of-war, I could tell Mom enjoyed watching me giggle with food in my hand.

"Okay, it's yours," she relented.

"Just kidding." I unveiled our brunch and pinched off a crumb for a taste.

"Corinne, you do have her at the top of your big sis list, right? She seems perfect for you." We both had no idea just how perfect Delaney would be for me.

For birthday dinner, Mom took me for my favorite meal: grilled fish tacos at the Lazy Dog Cafe. I could eat the fish and the cabbage, leaving the corn tortillas off to the side. We followed the hostess to a table full of friends who yelled, "Surprise!" The word didn't begin to describe those past few weeks.

I tried hard to act happy, and I was—in part. I counted myself blessed to have friends surrounding me, a school I loved, a sisterhood, and a life in

Southern California, back in the good old USA. But I struggled with birthday memories from the year before: a special trip to the States, Curtis' house and the breakfast he so attentively brought down to the guest room, eighteen yellow-stemmed roses from my dad, a special-delivery birthday cake from Mom, Curtis' football game the following day. He couldn't play that year, but I still cheered him on as he assisted the coaches on the sidelines. It had been an idyllic weekend. I fought the time travel between this year and that one, forcing down a couple of tasteless bites in view of my observant mother.

Memories continued to distract my senses, leaving me no time to indulge in the present. We all left the restaurant and headed for Chapman's stadium. That same evening, our Panther football team faced Whittier College. Excited about the 3–1 start to the season, the Chapman student body filled the stands to show their support.

I made it through the first quarter, but found the second more challenging. I couldn't do it. I couldn't sit there and listen to all the cheering fans. Their happiness suffocated me. Every yell, every chant reminded of Curtis' absence. I could no longer pretend I was okay. Anxiety set in. My breathing quickened. I had to get out of there, but I couldn't move the invisible someone sitting on my lap. The weight of my panic pressed down on me, pinning my legs underneath it. I looked to my mother who read my call for help.

"Corinne, I have to go to the ladies room. Would you show me where it is?" she asked.

I followed her to the side of the stands and down the steps, shaking in my new black leather jacket. Mom stopped at the bottom of the stairs and wrapped me in her arms, and as we stood there, I soaked in the faint memory of another hug—broad back, plaid shirt. We overheard campus security warn a student, "No reentry if you walk through the gate." Mom grabbed my hand and followed the student, the same warning reverberating behind us. I texted Sophe.

"We left for a sec and they won't let us back in."

It wasn't a complete lie. My mother and I silently strolled around the campus grounds, allowing me a reset before a small post-game gathering at the apartment of another sorority sister. Her sweet invitation for cake and a late-night toast was supposed to have been a grand finale to a daylong celebration. But as the clock struck twelve, I realized anniversaries had lost their meaning.

The following night my mom sat on the king-size bed in her hotel room while I worked at a nearby desk on a research paper based on the documentary *Thin*. She said she was checking e-mails, but she seemed strangely quiet.

"Mom, what? I know you." She looked up from her computer and stared at me as though considering what and how much information she should share.

"Curtis wrote me—wishing you a happy birthday," she said flatly.

He hadn't forgotten. But why not write to me himself?

Mom's eyes sharpened.

"I think there's something you should know. When you called and told me what happened between you two, I went into all your accounts and blocked Curtis and his parents. Both your e-mail accounts and your phone. I told him to leave you alone."

My head spun. *Maybe he did care and tried to get in touch with me after the breakup. Could that be why he e-mailed her and not me? Did he think I blocked him so he couldn't contact me? But wait, what? She has my password?*

By the look on her face, Mom had more to say.

Corbin had forgotten to log out of his Facebook account when he'd borrowed Mom's computer over the summer. My brother's friendship status with Curtis granted Mom access to my ex-boyfriend's timeline, providing her all the ammunition she needed.

"Corinne, sweetheart, you need to move on."

I couldn't look at her, and she couldn't hold her tongue from the pain she was about to inflict. I knew her attempt to change my denial into anger came from

199

good intentions, but my grieving process lagged far behind her expectations.

"He took someone on a date this weekend." My own mother twisted the spear lodged in my heart.

Sweat broke out on my hands. Hot liquid seeped under my tongue. I felt my pain drift away and a numbing cool sensation replace the beating in my chest. I wanted her to stop, but I also couldn't help my curiosity.

"Let me see." I looked at the open Facebook page.

Gray tie. Matching gray dress. All smiles. Curtis looked happy, and part of me was happy for him. She was pretty. The same girl appeared in his recent orientation pictures. I hadn't thought much of it at the time, but now I suspected she'd been the one who'd told me on the phone what a wonderful boyfriend I had. Had it been less than three weeks since the breakup? Our relationship spanned five birthdays and two proms. This celebration he shared with someone new.

The Dessert Dilemma

Over the following days, my mind sorted and compartmentalized thoughts into steel safety-deposit boxes. Memories of Curtis were sealed in a file labeled "Classified" with big red letters and locked up tight. I erased his looks, his voice, his words of promise.

Zazzy checked in on me and mentioned that Curtis had asked how I was doing. She wondered whether I wanted to know about him. My answer was, "No, nothing." I didn't care to know how he'd moved on and if he'd replaced me. I buried that part of me that included him so deep that retrieving any memory of him became an arduous task. I found it easier to process Curtis as someone I'd loved dearly who'd died suddenly. My concerned mother said she would stay in town for a while to make sure I was okay.

What happened next surprised me. A Pandora's box of sorts surfaced from my subconscious. I hesitated then unsealed it. Seductive whispers suggested taking a walk on the wild side. Bold, fun, euphoric Corinne let loose. Things I would never have done before, I did. What did I have to lose? The timing couldn't have been better. Sorority parties and meetings. Coffees with new sisters. Frat parties, football games, movie nights.

One day while I sat in the cafeteria with a group of girls, an older football player got up from his meal and walked over to me. He introduced himself as Granite. His arrogance intrigued me. We exchanged small talk and then he swaggered back to his seat. His triceps and tight T-shirt confirmed he spent quite a bit of time in the gym. Sharp angles on the jaw and piercing eyes. Yep, probably one of the best-looking guys on campus. I thought about it for a second. I wrote my name and number on a napkin then made my way toward him. As I walked by him, I slid the napkin under his plate and paused.

"See you later," I said.

He asked my name again, looking somewhat taken aback that I didn't remember his.

Granite Walker's name fit him on so many levels; he played defensive back for the Panthers during football season and took part in mixed martial arts fights as a side hobby. His Facebook status updates usually had something to do with the gym and lifting. To me, however, a spark of something even more appealing lingered underneath that firm surface. One night he texted me.

"Coffee and dessert at the Cheesecake Factory?"

Late-night coffee dates had become our thing, but not with dessert. My emotions raced over the idea of seeing him again. My eyes darted around the room looking for the express pass I must have received on leg one of this amazing adventure. *There must be a 'get out of dessert' pass here somewhere.* Approaching him the way I had in the cafeteria was way beyond my comfort zone, but I'd overcome the obstacle and won a date with the hot guy. Didn't that deserve some sort of reward? I replied to his text.

"Isn't that expensive?"

He must have sensed the underlying hesitation in the tone of my reply.

"Yeah, I would like to take you somewhere a bit nicer than where we went on our first date."

I recalled the Ugly Mug Cafe on Glassell, a late-night literary coffee house offering open mic nights for poetic performers. Granite knew what a girl wanted to hear.

"Besides, that means we can share something sweet."

I cursed my addiction to restricting.

I had mixed feelings as I sat in the passenger seat on the way to the restaurant. My palms began to sweat as I considered his appearance. His deep voice infected me. I had to look away. Steam from my mouth settled on the window's surface. I was overheating. I also felt a bit anxious—no, a lot anxious—figuring out a magical way of making cheesecake disappear. Over the last two years I'd mastered the art of hiding food from my family and friends, but venturing on this dessert outing elevated the game to a whole new level. One mistake might endanger future invites. I liked Granite and didn't want him to discover the albatross around my neck. But then again, I'd become more cunning since that dreadful day at Cinnabon.

We sat down at the restaurant and struck up a conversation. Granite surprised me by ordering not one but three pieces of cheesecake: original, vanilla bean, and chocolate. Great. It only confirmed how hard he worked out. Did he have even 8 percent body fat? I seriously doubted it.

Using conversation and sips of coffee, I shifted the attention from food to fitness.

"What does the 1200lb Club mean? Sorry, I stalked your photos."

He peered into my eyes and didn't answer my question.

"I kinda like you stalking me."

Suddenly his hands touched mine. They were coarse and muscular and showed signs of consistent wear and tear from heavy lifting. I took a slow, deep breath and hoped he couldn't feel the rapid pulse in my wrist. Raising my left hand, he turned the palm up to expose a film of sweat that threatened to give me away.

"What are you doing?" I asked.

He extended my fingers. I noticed how small and delicate mine were next to his.

"You have a ring on your middle finger," he said.

I smiled and thought of my father sliding that ring onto the third finger so long ago, asking me to keep it there until the day he walked me down the aisle. Dad wanted my husband to take off the ring.

I nodded and wondered where Granite was taking this conversation.

Mythology taking front and center, Granite described how the gods might characterize me according to the position of my ring and the lines on my hand.

His eyes captivated me. As he spoke, he seemed so sure of himself. My moral restraint treaded on shaky ground. He held all the cards of age and experience, tempting me into his lair with intellectual wit, which—I have to admit—excited me physically and mentally. I enjoyed the cerebral banter, especially since his error regarding the position of my ring gave me an unexpected edge. His misstep also made him even more attractive—exposed. I smiled wryly.

"Thank you. But it's on the wrong finger."

I slowly wedged the gold band from the middle finger, the only finger on which the ring could now securely fit. I glanced up and grinned, resting my ring on the original spot where my dad had placed it.

"It actually goes on this one. It's my purity ring."

A picture of me taken in Singapore when my ring still fit around my third finger. Not long after this photo was taken, I had to move the ring over to my middle finger. I'm cuddling my sweatshirt as I always did.

Unnerved, Granite changed course.

"You said you enjoyed the theater. Sometimes I drive up to Bakersfield and go with my family. We should go with them sometime."

Good move. He could process the bomb I dropped later.

Expertly multitasking, I listened intently to Granite. He said he had to leave the following weekend to watch his younger sister take part in a gymnastics competition. I held hawk eyes on him while I picked at my prey below, covertly dissecting graham cracker crust and cheesecake parts and distributing them around the plate. A sense of power surged within me as I surrendered without protest to my eating disorder.

I succeeded at the illusion of consuming what he might estimate as a satisfying amount for a health-conscious girl. I'd make up for the few bites I did have by not eating the following day. My sly technique needed no fine-tuning after all the times I'd practiced it. Granite paid the bill and we left. For the remainder of the evening, I soared with the unparalleled high of satisfying my anorexic addiction, knowing I could manage it without much consequence in all situations.

Slapped Sober

Several weeks had passed since the encounter with the girl in the waiting room outside of Susan's office. It was Friday, which meant I could relieve some stress by going out with friends. My goal during the weekends centered on ways to forget the past; easing back from my hectic weekday schedule allowed uninvited free time that sometimes led to unwelcomed memories. Parties and drinking offered gratifying diversions.

I'd made friends with some guys in what became my favorite fraternity. They lived in a house not far from my dorm, making it easy to find a party on any given weekend.

The theme for this particular night promoted dressing up as a high school stereotype. I put on my tight jeans, tube top, blue-plaid button-down shirt, and high ponytails. Reviewing that day's caloric intake, I confirmed the cushion I'd left for a night out. One shot of alcohol contained ninety-seven calories. I could get away with two, maybe three shots while pregaming at a girlfriend's house, and make my hyperactive buzz last until we reached the party. I could then top off the shots with a mixed drink and a snack and still be comfortable with my total calories for the day.

Doubting my memory, I recalled once again what I'd had that day so far: Vitamin Water Zero and an apple. I felt a little lightheaded, but that would ease off after my first drink. I promised myself that if I had more shots than my set limit, the following morning I'd wake up before my roommates and hit the track. I grabbed a pack of gum and headed out the door.

Walking through the crowded frat house, I hugged people from left to right. A guy dressed in a lacrosse jersey gave me a plastic cup of jungle juice and a thumbs-up. I started floating. A weight lifted off of my shoulders, not just because of the hard alcohol but because this place—with its rhythmic base and loud chatter—helped me relax. That's all I wanted. That and escape.

The alcohol dismissed the guard in my head and allowed me to eat, somewhat at my leisure. I grabbed a couple of chips and looked for a second serving of the potent punch. Making another round through the house, I noticed some friends and stopped to greet them. A moment later, I felt someone tap me on my shoulder. I turned around to see the long, blond hair that looked like mine, but I couldn't place the glamorous girl in front of me. I was tipsy, and she was a puzzle piece that didn't fit the disarrayed jigsaw stored in my jumbled brain. *Where have I seen her before?*

"Have we met?" I asked her.

"I've seen you before. You don't know me, but think of a place you might have seen me a couple of weeks ago."

I looked into her eyes. At first, they calmed me. Their color reminded me of crystal-blue lagoons I'd seen in the Maldives. Yet sadness loomed behind them. Then it hit me. I did know her. She was the girl who knew my secret.

I stood there gawking at her, speechless. I'd thought if I ever saw her again I would turn, put my head down, and dart away as fast as I could. I'd hoped never to face her or what she represented to me; I didn't want to be found out.

Time slowed until even blinking required effort. But surprisingly, I wasn't afraid. I stood my ground and didn't turn to avoid the truth. In fact, I did the opposite. I hugged her. I didn't know this girl. We hadn't formally met. Yet I opened my arms and embraced her—a total stranger, but not a stranger at all. She and I were sisters in hiding, held hostage by the same killer.

As I hugged her I could feel her shoulder bones hit my own. My arms wrapped around her fragile frame, my hands resting on her bony back. We held each other, and for the first time, I experienced what it must be like for someone to hold me. Bony. Tiny. Fragile. The physical awkwardness, however, didn't diminish our instant connection.

Releasing her grip, she took my hand and led me to an empty spot in the crowded house. We formally introduced ourselves and I learned her name—Grace. After initial small talk, her friendly tone turned earnest.

"Corinne, I need to tell you something and I want you to listen to me."

Her eyes became hard and fixed on mine. She squeezed my hand.

"I'm in congestive heart failure."

I'd been slapped sober. The blow landed across the right side of my head and caused a ringing in my ears. She went on telling her story while I recoiled from the strike.

"I'm being admitted to the hospital tomorrow, and I don't know when I'll be back."

"This happens?" I asked.

I was stunned. Suddenly the gravity of my illness became real. Grace could read my emotions as if she held the key to the hidden diary in my bottom desk drawer. As if to console me before the news became too weighty to bear, she continued on a lighter note.

"Hey, but before I go into treatment tomorrow, I'm living it up tonight."

Grace slurred her words. I focused in on her mouth, trying to follow her lips as she spoke.

"This is my night to have fun. I can worry about tomorrow later, but tonight, let's you and me forget about all this. Let's celebrate the fact we're here and living it up."

My thoughts were cloudy. Surely, I'd drunk way too much causing me to misinterpret her message. I also blamed the loud music. Maybe the noise had drowned out part of her story. I held onto her wrist to steady myself. I wanted to help her. But how? She grabbed my arms then held them hard.

"Corinne, this *is* real. You must get better. You have to get better. Promise me you'll get better. You don't want this."

I tried to focus on her gaze.

"I promise. But …"

Grace hugged me tight, turned, and dissolved into the crowd, arms up high, dancing to the failing beat of her own drum.

Facing My Monster

I wasn't sure how to cope with the news about Grace. It scared me. I think the news also scared my monster, sulking in its nebulous chamber. I'd read a quote about how a "good anorexic" is one who does not die. Maybe what I interpreted as antisocial behavior in my captor was instead a time of intense examination of that line between thinness and death. How far could my addiction progress before my heart failed?

I shared Grace's story with Mom who then moved to a hotel closer to campus. I told her to go home to be with Daddy, but she wouldn't have it. She said that she and my father were fine and that they agreed she should remain close by until my health stabilized.

I loved having my mom around, but I also found it a tad embarrassing. I finally had to ask her to pick me up down the street from my dorm so no one would see her. Sometimes I'd have to deflect a random question about her prolonged visits. I'd say she was seeing a friend. I didn't want to admit just how much I needed her, but I did need her. I needed her permission to eat. I constantly asked; she consistently answered. A simple yes would always do. Yes, I could eat. And yes, I could take small steps, but I had to take them. Somehow her gentle reminders soothed the sting of my oppressor, which for now remained somewhere in the shadows. For a while I existed on autopilot and tried not to think about Grace and focus on my studies.

To my amazement, my grades didn't suffer as much as I'd expected. Although I bombed a psych test the week after my birthday, my overall scores hovered above average. That's not to say I didn't struggle through that first semester. I did. But I also worked hard. If a professor had office hours, I made it a point to be there. I had marked on my calendar every extra point opportunity for attending lectures.

One speaker in particular captured my interest.

The poster publicized, "Holocaust Survivor Gerda Weissmann Klein to Speak at Chapman University, November 8." A recipient of the 2010 Presidential Medal of Freedom, Klein came to the school to impart her story of hope. Hope and freedom—two things I needed. I jotted down the particulars on my calendar and traced a big ink star several times in the margin.

I reached for my sweatshirt and notepad the night of Klein's talk and made my way to Memorial Hall. It turned out to be a popular event; a crowd had already gathered outside. *Glad I'm early.* When I entered the auditorium, Lindsey waved at me to come close to the front. I settled in next to her, iPhone off. I didn't want to be interrupted during this one.

"One Survivor Remembers" began playing on the screen. Atrocities of World War II and a final three-month death march. Klein had survived it all.

After the film, Klein came to the podium to speak. She both confused and amazed me from the moment I saw her, since neither her face nor her voice held any bitterness. The film mentioned how her weight had dropped to sixty-eight pounds and her hair had turned white due to lack of nutrition. But this woman before me had obviously lived a long and fulfilling life after a horrible period of captivity and torture. I considered her journey as she spoke of how she'd held onto optimistic imaginations: of fun and freedom; of throwing parties; of sharing strawberries and whipped cream with her friend. She told the audience not to focus on what is missing in life, but to see what is there.

How could this be? How could this woman keep anger and bitterness from taking root in her heart? And if she harbored no hatred—this woman who had experienced the worst of humanity—how could I, who hadn't experienced anything like that level of brutality, be justified in storing up resentment of my own?

I immediately turned in my mind and glared at my monster. I couldn't detect its form, but its presence permeated the darkness. So I waited and stood my ground. I didn't back down, but in quiet defiance I willed it to come out and face me. *How dare you!*

It was the first time I'd challenged my monster, but I sensed the rebellion of my action—and I liked it.

I tuned back in to Klein and listened to her example of turning trials into positive action. That gave me an idea. Maybe I could help others if I got well. Maybe I could come alongside girls like me and support them through their own struggles. As soon as I finished the thought, I realized the loftiness of that goal. My monster would not go away without a fight.

At that time my primary focus was on staying out of in-house treatment. But Klein's talk motivated me to envision a life beyond my current circumstances and try to act on it. I would aggravate my illness by taking a step toward recovery, but at least I had a strategy for counterattacking the enemy—a defiant face-off. Kinda sorta. Whatever the case, I no longer felt in complete submission. In fact, I started to grasp at hope—there might just be a way out of the torture.

Grace withdrew from Chapman on medical leave and entered a treatment facility. I didn't know if I could contact her, but I did anyway, not knowing if she would or could respond.

"I'm okay. Thank you so much for getting in touch with me. I should be out of here soon," she responded.

I imagined Ensure as part of her refeeding. Mom had asked me to inspect these complete balanced nutritional drinks at a grocery store. She'd said that she and my dad would do exactly what my nutritionist asked. If that required in-house care, they'd withdraw me from Chapman and I'd follow Grace's route of treatment. With 350 calories and eleven grams of fat per serving, Ensure was bound to be part of the program to gain weight. Drinking my calories did not sound appealing at all. I could think of many things I'd rather eat. I could have a Chipotle salad with barbacoa, black beans, and fresh tomato salsa for 320 calories and only eight grams of fat. I was not going in-house.

In the first week of December I began to prepare for finals. I also moved into a house with some sorority sisters: Sabreena, Christine, and my new big sister— Delaney! I was sure a fresh start in a new place could change everything.

Mom supported the idea and wanted to make sure I felt secure in my surroundings. So after I settled in, she took me to a nearby grocery store. With the help of my nutritionist's notes, I carefully selected the usual safe items and then added a few outside of my comfort zone. The food in my basket made me uncomfortable, but Mom's oversight kept redirecting me away from second-guessing my choices. When I finally spoke of feeling overwhelmed, Mom said we could stop. She smiled and looked as though she approved of my efforts. She praised me for my progress. Her words made me feel like I'd achieved something useful. I hesitantly approached the checkout lane and distracted myself by tallying the figures I was sure of:

> Sugar-Free Jell-O = 10 calories
> Small apples = 53 calories each
> Fat-free vanilla yogurt = 40 calories
> Swiss Miss Diet Hot Chocolate = 25 calories
> Vitamin Water Zero
> Del Monte dried apples = 110 calories
> Quaker Oatmeal Apples & Cinnamon packets = 130 calories
> Malt-O-Meal, 100-calorie packs
> Yogurt-covered pretzels, 100-calorie packs

The frozen waffles, bananas, and roasted chicken caused me a bit of distress, but I'd set my mind on making a change.

My turn in the checkout aisle. I placed my selections on the conveyor belt, averting my eyes from the box of waffles and resisting the temptation to read its nutritional panel. What I saw instead, however, didn't help. The cover of a popular magazine highlighted an A-list actress. She posed, all smiles and waving her hand. The headline taunted me: "Desperate to Be Skinny: She's surviving on just 600 calories a day." I zeroed in on the number. *I can beat that.*

I grabbed the offending waffles, the bananas, and the chicken and put them all back inside the cart. The actress looked happy enough to me. I chose sugar-free gum instead.

Mom just watched, dumbfounded, as I walked away incredulous and leaving Mom to pay the bill. A grocery store had just encouraged me to avoid food.

I went home and imagined making a YouTube health awareness video with me staring at a camera, summing up my experience:

I get high ... every time I step on a scale and record a lower number. I am your obedient daughter—the one you don't worry about. I cut out food groups for logical reasons. I work out and eat healthy; I'm disciplined. I set far-reaching goals. I am sick and dying right in front of you, but you cannot detect the killer inside me. Don't write me off yet—I am strong and determined. I will overcome this parasite that has engulfed me.

But you, media! You are also a parasite. You are a perpetuating factor in my illness, and I must also overcome you. When you report on the covers of your magazines that an A-list actress consumes six hundred calories per day, the anorexic in me says, "I can beat that." Where is your decency, your concern for her and for your audience? I will recover and I will be a voice. If you are suffering with this disease … (The National Eating Disorders Association symbol for recovery flashes on the screen.)

Minister Me

The first semester of my freshman year finally ended. College life hadn't been what I'd imagined. I desperately needed a break to regroup and believed time with family might soften my outlook regarding second semester—round two of what I assumed would be a continuing battleground for me. I decided to spend Christmas and New Year's Eve in Singapore. At least the magazines there with size-double-zero Asian cover models were sequestered in a separate section of Cold Storage, away from checkout aisles and potential panic attacks.

I eased through customs, and so did my disease. I found anorexia as harmful as drugs and bullets. They all kill. I couldn't seem to get a break. I needed a vacation from my head. Maybe alcohol and cute guys would do the trick.

Several nights of clubbing ended with a New Year's Eve finale.

"Ma. Is me." I tried not to slur, but it was no use. I forgot where I put my consonants.

"Corinne, where are you?"

"Inna taxi. Kin Daddy mee me dowstairs? I had muh-ney. Buh now is gone. I think the drinker people took it."

"Yes, honey, but stay on the line with me until you get here."

"I kinna wanna sleep."

"No, no! Stay on the line, sweetheart."

"Em-kay. How was ur ann-ver-sry."

"We had a great time. How about you?"

"I kiss Kristen's older bruther. His so cute. No big deal, though. K, ah-most home."

"Scott, she's here. Okay, Corinne. Daddy's on his way."

Dad met me at the cab.

"Hi, Petunia. Looks like you've had an interesting evening."

"Daddy!"

I was so happy to see him. He paid the fare and took my hand. The lack of activity inside the condominium's courtyard indicated New Year's Eve had come and gone hours ago. As I looked around for signs of life I lost my balance and fell, but before I reached the ground, my father picked me up and threw me over his shoulder.

"Daddy, Daddy! No, Daddy!"

I think the whole complex heard my voice and the contents of my stomach emptying down his back. We came through the front door of our third-floor flat to find Mom laughing hysterically. She'd heard us in the courtyard.

"Nah funny, Momma."

"I think it's hilarious. Go to the bathroom and I'll get you a cool rag and a change of clothes."

She apparently entered the bathroom to find me passed out cold next to the toilet. I later heard my brother and his friends had come in for a peek, seen the remnants of the rule-abiding little sister, and said, "It's about time."

I took a few days off from the social scene to recover before our family service trip to Cambodia. Mom had arranged a visit to an orphanage in Kampong Thom, a small village three and a half hours outside of Phnom Penh. The Shelter of Love, a nongovernmental organization for disadvantaged boys and girls, needed supplies and a fresh coat of paint. We volunteered to take provisions and contribute manual labor. I bought gifts for the girls.

Four pieces of luggage each carried fifty pounds of milk powder. Twelve tubs of Betty Crocker Rich and Creamy Vanilla Frosting, Mom's touch for the banana-cake demonstration, littered another bag that also contained our clothes.

I looked at the milk powder and the frosting that filled our bags and wondered what I could eat in rural Cambodia. The food choices around the shelter were probably limited, and I'd been told we'd eat with the kids. This was going to be hard. Maybe I could help out in the kitchen and set aside some veggies for myself. There had to be veggies of some kind.

As we flew to Phnom Penh, turbulence jerked the plane, so I studied the shelter's information packet to keep my mind occupied. The culture of Cambodia and the setting of the shelter called for modest but casual attire. The January climate guaranteed hot and dry weather throughout our stay. I noted a recommendation that any food items needing refrigeration be purchased in the city; items such as butter were scarce in the village districts. That idea—the scarcity of butter—put my mind at ease.

We didn't have any preconceived ideas when we arrived at the shelter and didn't want to play favorites, but it was hard not to shower extra attention on a little boy named Joshua. His grandmother brought him to the shelter the previous year and threatened to throw the malnourished and starving infant into the lake if the orphanage couldn't accommodate him. He had, up until then, lived on an insignificant portion of rice and water; in fact, Joshua had never tasted one drop of milk. All this had changed by the time we met him, and although his body was underdeveloped, his big smile and sweet nature made up for any deficit.

The goals of our trip included updating the shelter's roster with current photos, painting the trim on the boys' house, and baking banana cakes with some of the staff. I'd amended that schedule, adding a lesson on purity for the older girls. The plan was to give each girl a ring (the gifts I'd bought) as a reminder of the message. I gathered the rings and my lesson plan and approached the girls exactly as the training book says not to. I had the passion, but lacked the knowledge.

My agenda flopped. Some of the girls, including the newest arrival only two days prior, had come to the shelter already exposed to adult sexual matters. I hadn't expected that. I couldn't teach a lesson about purity given what many of these girls had experienced. A personal crash course in humility and improvisation took only moments. As I held the rings in my hand, the words came: "Wear this symbol, knowing you are loved."

During our stay, I learned about flexibility and the importance of building trust through relationship. My program was not important. Learning about the kids and their world—that's what truly mattered.

I listened to stories of hardship and survival that gave me more hope for enduring my own suffering. One girl's father had died of a snakebite. Her mother had a mental illness. Someone found the girl living under a plastic sheet at a market and brought her to the shelter. I heard many stories about the girls—backgrounds that included death, poverty, and desperation. And yet, here they were, sitting in groups on a porch and laughing in their free time while making friendship bracelets.

They inspired me with their strength and resilience. I'd come to minister to them, but in the end, they were the ones who ministered to me. They made bracelets for us and taught us their version of marbles. Those kids owned at marbles! Dad served as a human jungle gym. Mom gave lots of hugs. Before we left, a teenage boy presented Dad with a wooden carving that read, "Jesus Loves Scott & Family." Mom displays this treasured keepsake above the kitchen sink.

Home for the holidays in 2011.

The Puffin Affair

I returned to Chapman for my second semester with Mom by my side. I told my parents I had to see if I could make it on my own. She could stay for two weeks, but she had to leave after that. One early morning after a run, I brushed my fingers across the black bars separating the stadium from the athletic field. The predawn chill had started to lift, but the cold still nipped at my fingers. The run had cleared my head from a night of tossing and turning. Nightmares were an unusual occurrence these days but still made house calls now and again.

Spring was on its way. It refreshed me. I meandered past the almost-completed resident pool and then the dorm I'd stayed in as a first-semester freshman. I looked up. Not a cloud in the sky. An early morning chorus of chirping birds sounded as if they enjoyed the newness of spring.

I smiled. My mind and my body were waking up from their own state of hibernation with a fresh perspective. I could now look back on my first couple of months in college with an unobstructed view of the good as well as the bad. I'd spent a lot of that first semester managing my own triage. I'd repatriated to a home country not entirely familiar to me. I'd lost a twenty-eight-month relationship then watched as my weight cascaded to 79.8 pounds. I'd missed my dad, who lived on the other side of the planet and who was worried sick about me.

But I'd accomplished a great deal as well: rushing and joining an amazing group of girls in Gamma Phi, holding on to fifteen credit hours with a 3.0 average, avoiding in-house treatment. And I'd survived. I felt okay—in fact, better than okay.

I opened the latch to our gate and noticed a fresh rosebud on the patio bush.

"Hey, I'm home."

"Corinne, come here. Check out what I found."

Delaney popped her head over the back of our overstuffed couch. The excited yet cautious tone in her voice made me nervous.

"You've got your sneaky face on. Do I wanna know?"

Her face twisted into a smile as she announced, "I love Groupon."

"I don't trust you," I said.

"You can't be mad at me. And it's already done, anyway. It's a little too late to back out now."

She patted the vacant space next to her. I slowly moved to the couch and took a seat beside her.

"D, what have you done?"

"So, since we're going to San Diego with the girls for spring break, I thought we could get away and do something a bit crazy."

Her eyes widened as she held her hand over the computer screen, scooting the laptop toward me.

"Little sister, we're going skydiving!"

My mouth dropped.

"What? You're kidding."

She grinned and withdrew her hand, unveiling the coupon under "My Groupons" for Skydive San Diego, Inc.—marked "already purchased." I screamed and jumped up as if to run away from the words.

"Delaney! You know there are only three things I'm afraid of: calories, needles, and heights! No. No, no, no. No way."

I realized I wasn't the only one protesting as I paced around the room, making my impassioned plea. The voice inside my head amplified my argument, urging me to stand firm. Facing my fears—that wasn't part of the deal when anorexia and I became an item. Going for a run: fine. Working out: fine. Skydiving: not fine.

"Corinne, you need to break out of your shell." D's assuring, calm voice interrupted my inner dialogue. "You've been scared of things for as long as I've known you. This is your chance to prove to yourself that your mind can't control you."

She sat calmly with a determined look on her face, her elbows resting on her knees, hands folded and placed up to her mouth. Her eyes focused on mine. I looked at her intensely. I was mad at her, but she was right.

"Okay, I'll do it," I agreed, my voice quivering as I retreated to the shower.

Delaney smiled and snuggled back into the crevices of the couch.

"Ha. I knew you'd see it my way."

I went into the bathroom and shut the door. The fight raged on in my head. The monster told me I'd regret my decision. It started listing all the things that could go wrong. But part of me also didn't want to let D down—didn't want to let myself down. I'd said yes. I wouldn't go back on my word.

During college, a girl needs to break out of her cage of protection and solitude, spread her wings, and fall on her face a couple of times. In high school, I'd generally prided myself on being a caretaker for the more daring rule-breakers. I'd been pretty uptight back then. Now it was my turn to let loose.

The Chapman party scene meant music blaring, feet stomping, girls shouting. I could get used to this life. Guys dangled their feet over the sides of roofs. People arrived at parties and jumped fully clothed into backyard pools. New experiences, new situations, new people appeared around every corner. This liberal lifestyle appealed to my more mischievous side. I was committed to being open-minded, trying to figure out who and what I wanted to become.

Our nights out often began with my roommates at our house—nicknamed "The Hideout." Delaney, Christine, Sabreena, and I could be found in the kitchen chatting and laughing while other friends trickled in to join us for pregaming.

We'd raise shot glasses and congest our iPhones with Instagram uploads. As ten o'clock rolled around, one of us would impishly eye another and tiptoe toward a final swig of Honey Jack. Hesitating a second to compose ourselves, we'd tumble out of the door in tall high-heeled shoes and head for the parties.

Roommates at the Hideout:
Christine, Sabreena, me, and D.

"Guys, are you sure we're at the right place?" I asked.

The dark porch and quiet house seemed to hint that no one was home.

Julianne, who had heard of the party, hastily replied, "Yeah, yeah, yeah. This is the place! Let's go in the back way!"

"That doesn't sound a bit suspicious," I replied in jest.

She hurried to the side of the house and approached a tall white gate. The setting reminded me of Alice trying to find a way into an odd and secret place in Wonderland. If my college experiences so far were any indication of what lay ahead, I wouldn't have been at all surprised to enter a garden full of roses painted red.

As Julianne struggled with the latch, Melissa came alongside her, reaching over the gate to release the bolt. Our ears perked up as we heard the telltale click. The gate swung open and our mouths dropped at the site of an empty side yard. We looked accusingly at Julianne.

"No, wait! I swear this is this house!" she protested before absconding into the darkness.

Fearing that she'd become delusional and trespassed onto some stranger's property, we crept around the corner to retrieve her.

Bright lights flashed ahead. Thud. Thud. Thud. The beating sound kept rhythm with the lights.

Julianne was right; the party was here. The backyard led to a large patio and a sea of action. Twinkle lights draped the beams above, illuminating the scene as beer-pong players launched round orange balls into the air. People cheered as the balls hit a ring of red cups and bounced through the sudsy surface.

A deep, unfamiliar voice could be heard from within the mob.

"What's good?" asked a tall, muscular guy, donning a horse-head mask. He reminded me of a stallion posing for pictures after winning the Kentucky Derby. The mask completed him.

He must have seen the anxiety in our eyes because he let out a guffaw and took off the mask. "Oh, I'm sorry. My name is Zane."

"Hi! My name's Corinne." I smiled and held out my hand. The horse-man looked at my hand and shook his head.

"Naw," he replied.

He opened his arms and gave me a huge hug.

"Welcome to the party house! You and your friends are welcome to whatever you like. Drinks are in the kitchen, and if anyone gives you any trouble, you let me know."

Zane was a ladies' man, a fact evidenced by the amount of time it took for my friends to regain their composure.

Excited to explore the scene, I grabbed Sabreena's hand and led her through the stench of sweat and alcohol toward the kitchen. The effects from our pregaming were wearing off. We needed to top-up our buzz.

Alcohol lined the white-tile countertop.

"Choose your poison," Sabreena said, waving her arm over the rows of bottles.

I grabbed Jack. She chose Bacardi. We cradled the bottles and moved to the side of the counter, searching for clean shot glasses.

We noticed a commotion to our right. Two guys had pinned a large fellow upside down against a wall. Beer from a silver keg flowed into his mouth and spilled over his cheeks. I looked on, curious and amazed at how slowly the guys let him down after he seemed to choke on the amber liquid. He paused and shook his head while his buddies patted him on the back. Then he shot upward, let out a roar, and chest-bumped another guy to seal his success. I realized then that we were in a football house.

Football players at Chapman are a different breed—a clan of brazen and loud warriors. Being in with them meant being included in their Panther family. The idea attracted me.

"You girls look like you're looking for something."

I recognized the face of the guy who'd been upside down only moments before.

"What are your names?" he asked.

Perplexed, I measured his intimidating presence against his kind voice and gentle eyes. I considered his perfect posture then checked my own, pulling my shoulders back to mimic his stance. His husky build looked like that of a lineman.

"I'm Sabreena and this is Corinne. We're looking for some shot glasses." As Sabreena spoke, I studied his features. His big smile pushed his cheeks toward his eyes, making them squint—probably one of the cutest faces I'd ever seen on a guy.

"Well, let's get you two some welcome shots."

He drank Fireball and seemed happy to share his preferred indulgence with us. The taste reminded me of Red Hots, every sip sweet with cinnamon followed by a whiskey kick. It left a warm, tingling feeling in my stomach.

I slammed a few more shots and started feeling a little dizzy. I paused to count my intake. *Four shots. One too many.* As the alcohol took effect, my subconscious shifted its focus to food. The anorexia stumbled to find its oppressive rhetoric and failed.

I rummaged through the kitchen, opening cabinets and drawers, trying to find something to satisfy my drunchies. A cereal box on top of the refrigerator caught my eye. Shuffling my feet, I crept over, snatched the box, and slithered off to find a dark alcove.

I heard the kind voice calling after me, "Hey, wait! I poured you another shot!"

Revived from my stupor, I found myself settled in a corner on the patio, chewing slowly and sloppily.

"Hey, you okay?"

I looked up to find a six-foot giant standing before me. I tried to focus on his perfect teeth.

"Umm ... yeah. Yeah! I'm fine!"

My reply carried a hint of embarrassment. The way I'd been eating could have been mistaken for an adulterous act.

He chuckled. "Don't worry. Your secret's safe with me."

I bet anything would be safe with him.

"You look like you're in a hurry," I said.

"Yeah, yeah. I am, actually. I just stopped by after work to say hi to the guys. I'm working on a film and have to go do a shoot."

"Whoa, whoa, hold on. Wait a minute. Aren't you a football player?"

"Yeah, why?"

"You play football, you have a job, *and* you shoot movies?"

"Yes."

"How do you do all that? I hear the coach is pretty strict and you practice all the time, don't you?"

"Yes, but I'm also in Dodge—the film school? I wanna be a producer, and that takes a lot of work too."

"How do you manage all that?" I asked.

"It's all about balance. That's it. And hard work. But, yeah, balance. Hey, I gotta go, but you sure you're okay?"

"I'm better than okay. I have …" I looked down at the box. " … Puffins. Hee hee."

With a smile that belonged on a red carpet, he turned and disappeared into the crowd. But before he left, I caught a glimpse of his calm, sapphire eyes. *God, he's good-looking.* I tried to call after him, but cereal caught in my throat. And then he was gone. *Forgot what I wanted to say, anyway. But yeah, balance. That's nice. Oh well.*

The Puffins refocused my attention. I reached in the box to discover it empty. I'd eaten a half box of cereal. I thought of the words of wisdom spoken by the guy with perfect teeth. *Maybe balance is a good thing.*

Refueled by the influx of carbs, I threw down the box and stumbled back into the crowd.

The sun beat down on my eyelids, loudly knocking at the door of my consciousness. I responded to the annoyance by peeking at the ceiling. "Where am I?" I said aloud then sat up in bed.

Ouch! My head. I stared at a familiar lamp and framed photo. My brother's smirk in the picture echoed his words to me the first time I came home drunk: "Welcome to the wild side, little sister."

I looked around. I was alone. A sigh of relief escaped my throat, followed by a hiss as the throbbing sensation forced me to lie back down.

Surveying my room, I detected a trail of items leading away from my nightstand: skirt, black pumps, wallet, keys. I lifted the sheets to search for evidence indicating what had happened the night before. Still had on my underwear. *Thank God.*

I couldn't remember the final hours of the night or how I got home. *How long did I stay?* There was a vibration underneath my pillow. I retrieved my phone and saw a text from Jeremiah. *Who is Jeremiah?*

"Hey, how you doing?"

The text seemed sincere.

"I'm okay. How are you?" I texted back, hesitant.

"Do you remember who I am?" he asked.

I chuckled a little, wondering how long he would toy with my confusion.

"I'm so sorry, but no. I don't," I replied.

Almost instantly, he texted back.

"Lol. You said you wouldn't remember! You told me to text you in the morning to remind you to thank me for driving you home last night."

Disgusted with myself for letting a guy—no, a complete stranger—drive me home, I began to reprimand my behavior when another text appeared on my phone.

"Don't worry. We're just friends. We talked for two hours before I drove you home. Guys kept hitting on you, so I offered to give you a ride. Don't worry. Your friends made it home safe too."

Relief rushed over me. Even though I'd put myself in a bad situation, a sweet guy had managed to rescue me from my own stupidity.

"What did we talk about?" I asked.

"God. And how you felt terrible that you drank too much and danced on the table."

"Oh my gosh. I can't believe I don't remember any of that."

"It's fine. Really. We talked about this. You're a sweet girl."

"Thank you so much, Jeremiah! How can I repay you?"

"Be my friend and we'll call it even." He signed off with a smiley face.

Turns out that Jeremiah was one of the Panthers' star running backs. The guys respected him. And not just for his skills. His character and his kindness made him a standout on and off the field. And I'd been lucky enough to have him watch over me that night.

I could have seen that night as a failure, but I chose to see it as a success. I'd become aware that I was abusing alcohol to combat my controlling anorexic thoughts. Yes, I had unknowingly found a sneaky way of fighting the disease and silencing the torturous voices, but I had also exposed myself to the risks that go along with drinking.

So the voice can be conquered or at least subdued.

I just had to find another way—a healthier way—to shut it up.

"Corinne, what foods do you like?" Susan asked as she pulled out a slip of loose-leaf paper and attached it to a clipboard.

She must have known the mental strain her question would cause me. *Do I dare say Puffins?* She offered me the clipboard along with a black ballpoint pen. I glared at the floor. My cheeks turned hot. No one had asked me that question in such a professional setting. We'd discussed foods that were "safe" and foods that might be out of my comfort zone, but not foods I "liked." I hadn't considered what I liked for a long time.

I'd give lip service to my friends and say I liked a lot of foods. But I questioned the authenticity of my preferences. Was I covering for my illness, or did I truly enjoy things like French toast and pancakes? I ate them once in a while with friends to prove I could do it. But then I'd count the meal as a blow-it day and feel guilty afterward. Did I like to eat? I knew I didn't like the guilt and oppressive internal talk that followed.

Whatever foods I preferred, craved, or felt my body needed were usually on my prohibited list. My nutrition fixated on minimal sustenance—unless, of course, I was drinking. So my mind retreated to foods that made me feel safe: raw veggies, my lumpy-sawdust breakfast (otherwise known as Malt-O-Meal), or anything below one hundred calories.

I thought I liked that.

Susan then asked me to write down foods I'd love to try and to block out any negative connotations that might cloud my judgment. I tried hard and came up with four items: ice cream, pizza, avocado, and peanut butter. The idea of eating these foods without guilt existed far from the realm of present possibilities, but maybe this goal would keep my thoughts focused and hopeful. If I ever got out of my prison, I would love to eat them—without guilt. That was key: no guilt.

I envied people who could place items in a grocery cart without being bothered by calorie or fat content. To me, foods could be calorie-packed land mines. I envisioned myself waking up in the morning and exploding if I chose foods like pizza and ice cream.

I avoided these traps at all costs. *What makes Susan think I can do this now?* The exercise at the grocery store had been a complete disaster that addressed only a few items outside of my comfort zone. *Now we're discussing foods I like?*

When I finished making the list, she eased my mind.

"Okay, Corinne I don't want you to worry. You won't have to eat these things right away."

I sighed with relief as the tightly stretched rubber band inside my chest released.

She added, "However, you will eat them eventually."

My eyes stared into Susan's, trying to read her. *What does "eventually" mean? And does she mean without guilt?*

Next she asked about the Chapman cafeteria. We agreed on this familiar environment to begin adding foods to my diet. Together we came up with two menus. I labeled one "To Try," the other "Untouchables." By the end of the exercise, we'd created a meal plan.

I forced myself into the cafeteria for regular feedings. Ownership of the goal made the difference. I promised my nutritionist; I promised myself. I still avoided pasta, meat, and anything with sauce. I chose more fish and veggies. I added sweet potatoes. I added chicken.

Outside the cafeteria, I made sure I ate snacks between meals. I avoided binging on alcohol. I focused on variety in my food choices, in my schedule, and in my free time. Every time I felt tempted to veer away from the plan I repeated positive reasons for recovery.

One morning on the way to school I noticed discomfort below my rib cage. I pushed the aching sensation to the back of my mind and continued on with my day, but by 9:30 a.m., my thoughts were consumed with the strange and growing nuisance inside me. As I walked to another class, I passed

Jazzman's, a coffee shop on campus. My nose picked up the strong, sweet smell of toasted bread, hickory ham, and bubbly cheese. The smell of breakfast was not new to me, but the grumbling in my stomach was. Startled, I realized the feeling might be hunger.

Instead of giving in to the craving, I darted to my next class, trying to make sense of the change. I'd had breakfast at 7 a.m. Why would my body already be hungry? For so long, my mind controlled my emotions as well as my physical needs, suppressing cravings and appetites. Now that I'd begun processing my emotions with my psychologist, my body responded by processing its physical needs. It started feeling again. Feeling hunger. I can't say I was happy about it. What I felt was disappointment and confusion.

As the gurgling in my stomach increased, my eating disorder screamed at me. *Look what you've done! All our progress wasted! Go ahead. Gain pounds and be vulnerable! All you'll have is pain! Pounds and pain! You'll be fat, ugly, and weak!*

The mental bullying continued throughout my next class. I couldn't focus. After class was dismissed, I covered my ears with my hands and walked out of the room. I rushed to the bathroom and barricaded myself in one of the stalls where I sat down and rocked back and forth, counting the footsteps of others coming in and going out, trying to soothe myself and calm my shaky hands.

After a while I looked at my phone. Twenty minutes had flown by. I opened my eyes, and cupping my face in my hands, I took a deep breath and reminded myself why I wanted to get better: to be free from the chains of anorexia, to go out and eat with my friends, to feel happiness, to run without fear of collapsing with a strained heart, to stay awake for more than five hours at a time. As I counted the positives, the tormenting voice of the eating disorder quieted, and I suddenly realized I'd regained control of my thoughts.

Hunger took center stage once again as the tightening and churning in my tummy returned. My body acted like a toddler demanding gratification. I determined to retrace my steps to Jazzman's where I decided I'd grab something to tide me over until lunch. I reached for nonfat Greek yogurt and an apple (my current go to snack/lunch) but then decided to make a small change. I grabbed a banana instead.

Moving from an apple to a banana may seem like a small step, but anyone suffering with anorexia would know otherwise, especially since I'd chosen to eat the banana on my own. To my anorexic mind, the glucose levels and calories in the two fruits are massively different. The option of having a banana was not one I would have considered before treatment. Bananas bordered on the impossible. But I knew I couldn't remain stagnant if I wanted recovery. I had to keep making progress.

I peeled the fruit and took a bite. I repeated over and over the reasons for eating. "I want to be with my friends." "I want to have energy." "I want to sleep when I'm supposed to sleep." "I want a healthy heart." "I don't want to be cold all the time."

"I want recovery."

Freedom in Falling

B y spring break, I'd become quite comfortable talking back to my monster. Although there were still many times I felt inadequate during the arguments, my positive rebuttals placed me in a rising position of strength. And as I became stronger, I realized I could confront my other fears as well, including that of heights. Time to cash in on that skydiving Groupon.

Delaney, one other friend, and I made our way to a small airport one morning to jump out of a perfectly fine plane—something I wouldn't have done a few months earlier. Two days before, five of us packed into two cars and drove to San Diego for spring break. Now three of us had a rendezvous with the most daring adventure I could imagine. The two smarter friends remained at the hotel.

I was still restricting and hid my illness during our trip—thanks to our vacation mode of sleeping in late and eating on the go—but the anxieties surrounding the physical act of eating took a back seat to the emotional encounters that were paving the way toward recovery.

As I peered into the clouds, I hoped and somehow expected one of them to change shape into a heart or a thumbs-up sign—anything indicating a good outcome to this idiotic decision. *How did I let her talk me into this?*

Suddenly I noticed three dark specks in the sky, tiny blemishes on a vast powder-blue-and-white canvas. Squinting and with the curiosity of a cat observing a fly, I studied their haphazard pattern. The specks expanded as glints of light ricocheted between them—sunlight reflecting from a metallic wing above the floating objects. My eyes soon registered the silhouettes as people dangling from horseshoe-shaped parachutes.

As kids, Corbin and I tossed toy paratroopers from a fort in our backyard. Now was not the time to think about karma; those green men had not landed softly all those years ago.

My stomach dropped. The scene above me would be our destiny in a few minutes.

The car changed gears as we moved from smooth pavement to uneven gravel. My eyes scanned our surroundings, but trees blocked my view. I looked at Delaney. Nothing fazed her.

The landscape opened abruptly, changing to lush, rolling hills in the distance. Beyond the hills were mountains, and against that backdrop a soft grass platform came into view—our landing field. We turned onto a path that led to a large, open area. A small aircraft awaited our arrival. Two instructors approached our car. Delaney parked and rolled down the window.

"Hi, my name is Delaney Starks and we're here to skydive."

She stepped out of the car and handed them some paperwork. She'd known not to ask for my help filling out the forms, with their small-print scenarios of "bodily injury and/or death." I sat in the car with my seat belt still buckled around me, watching warily as my friend chatted nonchalantly about our impending doom. The instructors turned to leave. *Maybe they told her we can't go up today. Nope; no such luck.* Delaney's head whipped back in my direction as she waved for us to get out of the car. *No going back now.*

My hands began to shake, making it hard for me to depress the red sliding pin on the seat-belt buckle. After three fidgety attempts, it clicked. My last excuse—gone. I wobbled after Delaney, signed away my life, and donned a blue jumpsuit.

"Hello, my name is Aidan," my instructor said. "I'll be your free-falling buddy for today."

You are not my buddy. I figured the sooner we got this over the better. I focused on the brightness of his slick head—anything to distract me from the logistics of the jump.

"Corinne, all you're gonna be responsible for today is your arms and legs. Keep your arms and legs out and you'll be fine. If you don't … well let's not get into that. Keep them out and I'll do the rest. You think you can do that?"

His words sunk in like a death sentence. As the blood drained from my face, I nodded without a word.

"Atta girl!" He planted his hand on the center of my back with a thud, leaving me breathless.

We climbed into the plane, and as we took off, nervous excitement filled the cabin. I peered out of the window to a spectacular sight, the earth in all her beauty. For a moment I forgot my objections and admired the scenery: textured shades of brown and green with a few splashes of liquid blue. Hypnotized by God's majesty, I soaked in the wonders of creation until a booming voice interrupted my state of tranquility.

"Ladies, we're now over thirty-seven hundred feet. Get ready to jump!" It was Aidan.

After my so-called buddy made his announcement, he directed a few commands at me. "Corinne, we're going first. I'll count to three and then we'll jump."

The door slid open. A gust of ice-cold air brushed my face. My body shuddered against Aidan's as I sat strapped to his torso.

"All righty then, here we go," he said.

His calm demeanor annoyed me. He rose to his feet. My body followed. My knees buckled in dissent, but his legs were stronger, rousing mine into forward march.

"Aidan, I'm scared!"

He smiled and looked down at me.

"Don't worry. I've got you! Now listen! You've got to hang out of the plane while I hold this metal bar and count to three. Okay?"

My mouth opened wide.

"You're going to be fine. I promise!"

Aidan's coaching nudged me forward, and as he held the bar I dispatched my clumsy legs out of the craft. I looked down. I shouldn't have done that. Wind, the first obstacle, slammed my legs to the side. I fought to hold my position.

"One!"

My heart seemed to stop and then restart.

"Two!"

I closed my eyes and waited for "three."

We dropped.

Falling backward, I reached out for the safety of the plane. Do-over! *He didn't say three!* My stomach lurched ahead of me as we plunged into fate. I was afraid, but I was also infuriated. *What a liar!*

The wind tossed me around like a rag in a storm. I hugged myself for comfort, but Aidan grabbed my arms and extended them. I remembered the only thing he'd asked of me: "Keep your arms and legs out and you'll be fine."

I followed his instruction, but fear still gripped me. *I'm gonna die. I'm gonna die. I'm gonna die.*

Until I realized that maybe I wasn't.

Prayer came to mind, and as my thoughts refocused, the wind switched sides, becoming my ally. High-pitched screams turned into uncontrollable laughter. I began to notice the allure of the amphitheater below when I realized we'd reached terminal speed. The acceleration had stopped. I was free falling—free and falling.

The sound of my mood change must have signaled my instructor, who set out to give me the ride of my life. Right spins. Left spins.

I felt a tap on my shoulder, a signal for me to brace myself. The hissing sound of a string projected skyward. The wind caught the trailing material, unfolding a canopy that gently escorted us to the landing field. I continued laughing as tears began to drop on my airtight goggles.

"I guess you had fun then?" Aidan said, chuckling.

We drifted to the ground with vitality and rebirth filling my soul. I'd faced fear head-on and conquered it. Me. Afraid of heights. Afraid of falling. Afraid of life itself. One little act of defiance against my better judgment invigorated me—and showed me I'd been wrong. My paradigms for fear and life could be altered.

I cheered as D landed. I loved her for making me face my cowardice. I'd remember this day—and not only for the grand feat of jumping out of a plane, which I actually wanted to do again. No, on this day I'd opened up to another opportunity of hope. Hope for bravery. Once my feet had touched that lush, green grass, I knew I could fight fear and win. If I could overcome this fear, maybe, just maybe, I had within me enough courage to conquer my weaker self.

Me and my big sis.

Time to Grow Up

T he end of my freshman year approached. How in the world had it gone by so fast? I thought about the wisdom I'd gained from the people I'd met over the course of that year: the reality of consequences from Grace; the benefits of vision and gratitude from Gerda; the value of community from the girls at the shelter; the empowerment of courage from Delaney. Each lesson added layer upon layer of the confidence I needed to free myself from addiction.

The Spring Formal brought a change in my social life. I decided to go with my best guy friend. On the way home, he stopped walking, and out of the blue, he kissed me. The chemistry between us produced a new bond; I began to see him in a different light. He was funny, outgoing, and he was here. I wouldn't have to manage this relationship from afar—a huge plus in my dating handbook. Actually, he lived in the house next to mine. Couldn't get much closer than that.

We were, on the other hand, polar opposites in our backgrounds, interests, and the way we looked at life. That didn't matter to me, at least not at the time. Michael promptly answered my texts. He arrived early for dates. For me, this would be an easy transition from friends to … hmm, not sure what.

Mom and Dad made summer plans to come over from Singapore and included a family trip to Yellowstone and Devils Tower. The four of us would meet in Denver then drive to Vail so my parents could recover from jet lag. That made me a little uneasy. Was I ready for Colorado? This would be the first time I'd be back in the stomping grounds of memories I shared with Curtis. California was safe. Curtis and I didn't share a thing in California. But to land at Denver International Airport, travel through the city, and walk into a house where I'd spent that last evening with him before we went off camping?

I bit my lip—hard. Mom said we'd take I-70 straight to Vail. I'd have an opportunity to make new memories at the house. We'd be there only a couple of days before heading to Wyoming.

I posted our plans on Facebook and soon after saw a "like" from Zazzy Brown. Zazzy. Forgot about Zazzy. Skilled in the art of diplomacy, she ended up as one of the few friends in the "Both" column after the breakup. I wanted to catch up with her but didn't want to think about Curtis. Still, I needed to thank her for helping me the previous winter.

Back then my weight had spiraled down once again as the stress of fall finals triggered a spike in my restrictive behavior. Zazzy kept reaching out to me, trying to talk and Skype, but I was preoccupied with reinforcing another wall around myself. I'd canceled plans and Skype sessions with friends, choosing instead to spend time with my mother or alone—isolating myself in the confines of my illness.

Zazzy called me out on it, telling me I couldn't shut out those who cared about me. I didn't like what she'd said, but her candor persuaded me to consider how my friends must have felt: reaching out to someone who seldom reciprocated; making plans only to have them canceled at the last minute. Her words were powerful and true, and they stuck. As a result of her counsel, I decided to make a sincere effort at reconnecting to the world around me.

Yes, I'd have to see Zazzy. But, I could think about that after the trip.

The next two weeks were spent rediscovering the wonders of creation and the relationship with my brother, all instigated by an unexpected late-May snowstorm.

We'd arrived at Old Faithful in time to see the famous geyser live up to its name by erupting on schedule. Corbin and I ran to pose for the photo op. Dad's camera captured the moment I kissed my brother's cheek. I checked the photo to see my twin; Corbin's eye twinkled and the corner of his mouth revealed a slight grin.

After the display was over we walked to the car, arm in arm, my brother and I. Snow showered the parking lot in large, bountiful flakes. We approached our parking space; I noticed a tour bus blocking our car. I chuckled knowingly at the white flag waving above a line of camera-toting tourists. I heard familiar sounds—an Asian language. The black-clad visitors bowed and apologized. We caught ourselves unaware, bowing back several times until they boarded the bus.

As the driver pulled away, the four of us stood and looked at each other. We were different now. In our home country, inside the oldest national park, where the vibrant color combinations of rock formations reflected humanity's melting pot, I realized my family had grown together and with the world. What had bothered us before moving overseas, before depression, before anorexia, before separation, didn't bother us as much anymore. The annoyance of things like parking lot dramas seemed trivial compared with the smiles of apology and acceptance. We'd evolved.

That beautiful cold and delicate snow accumulated and created a pause in our lives, closing the roads and gifting us with a shift in our plans. Dad managed to book a room at the Old Faithful

Inn—something he'd tried to do six months earlier without success. "Fully booked." Now we'd been awarded the blessing of remaining in the park an extra day with the chance to wake up at the break of dawn to see the geyser erupt one more time. The morning show promised a more private affair, since few people wake up as early as my father and I. That night I learned that happiness comes to those who can roll with life—who can accept each other not only in spite of faults, but for them. I learned that change is okay. I would be okay. My family would be okay.

"Corbin, stop it!" I laughed as I tapped out from our tickle fight. We calmed down and cuddled as if there had never been a rift. So many times, magic arises out of what seems impossible.

When we arrived back at the house, my attitude had changed for the better. Corbin kept me occupied with paintball skirmishes around the property. Mom made sure we were all geared up with masks, adding some extra padding up top for me. I later thanked her for that—Corbin had no mercy.

Dad mentioned the Rockies were in town. We planned a family outing to the Saturday game and invited Zazzy to come along. I asked her if we could meet at the main entrance to Coors Field. I made up an excuse for why we couldn't pick her up on the way to the game. I hated lying to her, but I had to keep a safe distance from Curtis' neighborhood. Zazzy lived too close to my past, and after all, reconnecting had its limits.

I have no idea about the stats for that game. I'm not even sure which team the Rockies played. Zazzy and I talked the whole time to the apparent displeasure of the fans sitting behind us.

Me and Zazzy at the Rockies game.

Zazzy is enamored with all things British. She's obsessed with Princess Kate. She fancies afternoon tea. *Downton Abbey* is her favorite show. I have no doubt she will someday settle in England given her drive and determination. We gabbed about college, her theater classes, my sorority, and the new guy in my life. It wasn't until we exited the ballpark that the topic turned to Curtis. I became quiet and took a deep breath.

"He asks about you."

She said he enjoyed living in Chicago. He'd joined the rowing team and a fraternity—the same one as my brother. She mentioned he felt bad about the way things had ended between us. After that, I tuned out. I appreciated the sensitivity and optimism in her approach, and it had been 8 months since the breakup, so why the constriction in my throat and the numbing sensation in my legs? Why did I care that her briefing didn't include an indication that Curtis missed me?

I told Zazzy that I wished him well and that he shouldn't worry about how we ended. I'd moved on. I resolved not to entertain any more thoughts of him. *I'm okay. I'm okay.* I had to keep reminding myself the night was almost over.

We all spent the next thirty minutes in the car making concentric circles around lower downtown (LoDo), trying to find Union Station. We'd planned on dropping Zazzy off at the train bound for the Dry Creek stop where someone from her family would be waiting for her. That goal, however, proved elusive. The trendy restored historic district of Denver apparently forgot to include directions for part-time visitors. Despite our best efforts, five people navigating one-ways and right-turn-onlys could not reach the train station, a building we could see. And our car was running on fumes. Our goal shifted from getting Zazzy home to making sure we all got home. Pulling into a gas station, Mom ran in for Sugar-Free Red Bull and cherry sours. When she came out, she addressed Dad at the pump then opened the car door.

"We're takin' Zazzy girl home," Mom said as she hopped back onto the front seat then turned to see our reactions.

Corbin and Zazzy yelled, "Yes!"

I froze. *Uh-uh. No. No way. Cannot go there.* I looked at my mom, terrified, letting her read me loud and clear. That part of town was not an option. She raised her eyebrows and shoulders at the same brief moment as if to say, "Honey, you can do this."

No, I cannot do this! Please don't make me do this.

My eyes welled up as I prepared for a psychological attack, but my defenses had already been compromised and I could only watch in horror as boxes of memories dusted themselves off and unlocked.

I wanted to avoid I-25 at all costs. That highway connected me to Curtis' neighborhood (the high school he attended, restaurants, movie theaters, stores, parks—all memories of ours).

Thank God Zazzy and Corbin were chatting up a storm, unaware I'd checked out. Mom kept her back to me in the front passenger seat, while Dad periodically glanced in his rearview mirror, reflecting my pain on his face.

Daddy. I'd forgotten about the burden he carried. Mom had let me in on a one-sided confrontation Dad had with Mr. Alexander. It happened one day in a lodge at the base of Copper Mountain. Six of us were taking a break from tubing and the cold: Curtis and me, our fathers, and Curtis' twin sisters. Curtis and I sat at one table, the dads at another. The twins were off searching for hot chocolate. The conversation between the dads turned to us. My father began by offering his continued support for the relationship Curtis and I shared.

"You know this can never last," Mr. Alexander said, turning his head toward the voices of his advancing daughters. Dad, taken off guard, didn't know how to respond. He told Mom he'd been surprised and confused by Mr. Alexander's apprehension. Curtis, however, had reassured my father soon after, pointing out the special nature of our relationship and saying he wanted to make it work. Dad approved of my boyfriend—not an easy thing to do for a protective father. I knew he blamed himself now for not acting sooner, for not recognizing the weight of Mr. Alexander's message.

The memory of that conversation made me wonder how long Curtis' dad had been against us. I'd always praised and encouraged Curtis by saying, "You're so much like your dad." Had I inadvertently assisted in setting up the plot—the one that led to Curtis using his father's exact words in our breakup?

We pulled into Zazzy's driveway. I feigned excitement as we said our good-byes and exchanged hugs. The car door shut and I allowed the tears to flow. Mom asked if I had a preferred escape route. It didn't matter now. Any direction from her home harbored spirits of the past.

I stared out of the window with eyes of stone, quietly accepting the beating from familiar sights. I tried to calm myself by counting my slow intermittent breaths. The intersection of Highway 470 and I-70 finally brought some relief. There, I promised myself not to return to Denver until I could associate my memories of Curtis and me with a smile.

I needed to grow up. No more fairy tales. No extremes. No tragic play. I wanted what everyone else seemed to get and I had yet to grasp. I'd kept making wishes upon stars and believing Disney films were real. I'd been expecting too much from myself and way too much from others. People mess up. Friends and family hurt each other. Journeys collide and then depart. A promise broken doesn't mean it lacked sincerity. And seasons shouldn't be mistaken for more than what they are: temporary.

Visiting the past had aroused a rude awakening in my perceptions of life, but it also set in motion another turning point in my recovery. I wanted to be well and knew I had a lot of work to do. The help I searched for called me back to its source—California, my new environment, my home. I informed my disappointed parents of the change in plans. I was breaking away from them and from the need to please everyone. I was making my own decisions now. The Rockies game was on the second of June. I flew home two days later.

Since my first experience of being alone—left inside my mother to push against her pelvis as well as against the unknown—I'd lived in a state of purgatory awaiting permission, or forgiveness, or acceptance.

I needed freedom. Freedom to explore. Freedom to make my own mistakes. Freedom to allow others to make theirs. Freedom to have opinions that didn't match those of my family or my friends.

I returned to Orange in time too see Fourth of July decorations drape the square. The roundabout displayed flags and banners in support of those who'd served our country. I love this small town—where people know their neighbors, reach out to their community, and ground themselves in the joy of living. Chapman embodies that feeling for me as a place where I walk across campus and say hello, where I reach out and serve those in need, where I practice being grateful regardless of my circumstances. Here I became acquainted with the adult me. And I like her. She is strong, resilient, recovering. I found only one drawback to my growing independence.

As I got better, my relationship with my mother deteriorated. My contact with her dwindled from three frantic consultations per day—asking if I could eat an apple for a snack or if frozen yogurt would be all right after dinner—to one courtesy call per week. She suffered major withdrawals. There were fights, Mom worrying about my weight and our lack of communication.

I regretted the emotional distance and missed talking with her, but I'd finally recognized the legacy and dangers of our codependent relationship. I couldn't rely on her so much, and she couldn't fix everything. We needed a reset.

During that time I began to search outside myself. I wanted to shift the focus from me to others. I had learned about poverty and hardship, the down and the destitute, while living overseas. However, I never quite understood the level of misfortune that existed in America until after I moved back. The world believes that everyone in the United States is rich. And we are, comparatively speaking. A third of the world lives on less than two dollars a day. But I found a lot of hurting people in my own backyard as well.

I'd heard that Rock Harbor Church had recently opened a satellite campus—a five-minute walk from my house—so I visited one Sunday morning shortly before the start of my sophomore year. Friendly volunteers providing information lined a walkway leading to the auditorium. A cheerful voice from behind one of the tables said hello and asked if I'd like to come to a potluck.

"We meet up every first Sunday of the month with local homeless families in need. It's not far. You should come."

On a sunny day in Hart Park, parents and kids surrounded picnic tables piled with salads, chips, cookies, and baked beans. The smell of burgers on a grill lingered in the air. I approached a volunteer, introduced myself, and my made-from-a-box brownies then found a place to sit next to a thirty-something mom with two kids. We introduced ourselves and started chitchatting. She was pretty, hair long and combed, face slightly tanned, no makeup.

"What's the hardest thing about being out here—about being homeless?" I asked.

She looked like she didn't get the question often. She didn't have to think long.

"Taking a shower, for sure." I cushioned my neck on the palm of my hand and thought about the shower I'd taken before I came to the park. My head began to race, thinking about what living must be like for her. *How does she find a job if she's dirty? How do the kids go to school with the added social stress of a scent that reeks of homelessness?* "I can find a meal," she explained, "but if we use a public shower, I could be fined, and it's a big fine."

I looked into her eyes and digested what she'd said. Could this be true? I used the restrooms at the beach all the time. Many people showered there. I'd never noticed homeless people taking a shower, but I wasn't looking for them either. I recalled girls in bikinis, families washing down boogie boards, and people putting on a fresh change of clothes. My memories didn't include anyone who looked homeless, though. Would I even know if they were?

An awareness washed over me as a stone lodged itself in my gut. For a moment, I reverted to my old impulse of placing her burden on myself. Maybe I could be her Good Samaritan and find a way to get her a shower when she needed it; maybe she could shower at my house. *Wait.* I thought I'd heard of some organization or charity that offers portable showers for the homeless. And it wasn't far! Dana Point, I think. I'd read that one of the charity's challenges involves storage of the shower units. With all the homeless people in the area, couldn't the units always be in use?

I caught myself. I'd begun obsessing over the shower dilemma. Obsessing leads to anorexic thoughts. I had to focus. *Be present, Corinne.* What could I, in my current state of healing, offer her? Friendship is what came to mind. Two girlfriends confiding in each other on a park bench, laughing and talking and being present in the moment.

Indeed, part of my recovery required me to focus on the present and not to worry so much about the future. It also encouraged me to watch for destructive patterns in my behavior. My efforts were paying off, as I noticed an increase in my ability to redirect my thoughts when they started to spin. My goals were to enjoy each moment, to concentrate on being present, and to leave the past and the future where they belonged. Once in a while, though, this exercise still proved futile, especially when dealing with the past.

Fall football quickened my step around campus. I couldn't wait for the games to start. I was a sophomore girl dating a senior wide receiver. What a difference from the year before—a full year since Curtis and I broke up. And although my mind discouraged revisiting memories of us, I was able to forgive Curtis for leaving me. I couldn't fault him for our diverging paths. For some strange reason, though, I'd felt driven to pray for him lately and wondered why. I'd sometimes send up a short request, wishing him well, but every once in a while the intensity of the prayer would hit me hard. Finally, I could no longer ignore the nagging at my heart. I had to know if he was okay. And I'll admit it: I also wanted to see if we could salvage anything from what we'd shared.

I wrote him an e-mail on October 7. My birthday passed, and so did the expectation of any response. A few more days went by before I spotted an inbox message from his address. I couldn't open it right away. First, I had to process some feelings. Did my Tristram have soothing words for me from beyond our relationship's grave? All the what ifs and maybes started driving me crazy. So impulsively, I clicked over his name.

A frosty and uncomfortable sensation surfaced as I read the opening sentence of his reply. He began, "Corinne, my long-lost friend."

He apologized for how things had ended between us. He didn't want to go into detail, but realized his actions had been out of line. He said he'd cherish the place in his journey that was uniquely ours and that his conscience had been comforted by my reaching out. He asked about my year at Chapman.

The message ended, "God bless, Curtis."

My imagination had conjured up various scenarios of making amends, but not this one. The reserved diction included cliché formalities that might as well have been sent with a translation option. The tone, devoid of anything resembling my first love, made me suspect *my* Curtis no longer existed; at least he wasn't there. Whoever replied—whoever forged these words—didn't even know Curtis. No, this had to be an impostor. I read the message one last time, knowing I wouldn't respond. Calling up the dead had extracted a price I didn't wish to pay again and only confirmed what I'd already known to be true in my heart. My knight. My prince. His memory of me had changed just as mine had of him. That part of my life was over.

Flashbacks of us filled my mind. What we'd shared. How we'd grown. The tokens we'd exchanged. CDs storing our songs, labeled with phrases that belonged to no one but us. An unblemished shell he brought me from Sanibel, his high school photo ID, ticket stubs for the Denver light rail, and a solved Rubik's cube. Neon-yellow sunglasses with "2011 Prom" stamped on the frame, bracelets that had accidentally broken, necklaces he'd made for me out of hemp, and wristbands. Christmas ornaments, cards that had come with fresh flowers, cards from his sisters and his mom, poems, a program from the Renaissance festival, and the first postcard he'd written me from his summer camp. Sticky notes listing my nicknames (Goldfish, Angel, Princess, Sugar, Hippo—because we made a funny face together) and another with our unique postscript, xoxstar/0. A sample vial of his cologne, the only remnant of his scent.

Mom stores these things at our home in Singapore, far away from my curiosity and random weak moments. Someday I know I'll have to collect these crumbs of us and toss them into a dustbin of indifference. But I'm not ready to erase the trail leading back to what once had been my safe place. That can wait.

I needed my mom. At two o'clock in the morning her time, she picked up the phone.

"Hi, Mom. Curtis wrote back."

She cleared her throat, more alert.

"His mom wrote to Dad and wished you a happy birthday," she said.

Her words surprised me. I had mailed some sentimental items of Curtis' to his parents back in January; I even sent an e-mail to his dad telling him to expect a box from me. I never heard they'd received anything.

Mom continued, "Corinne, honey, do you need closure?"

Closure. So final. I pictured seeing him again. Wow. The last time I'd seen Curtis was the night at the campsite. I shook the memory away. No, that could never happen—seeing him again. I thought about talking with him on the phone. I'd erased the sound of his voice. The last time I'd heard him speak he'd begun the conversation by saying he loved me— on the phone—the day we broke up.

I didn't think I could bear hearing him address me as that long-lost friend. We weren't friends. And besides, I was dating someone else. It wasn't in my nature to stray, even in my thoughts. Maybe texting or e-mail? Reaching out to him had already proved awkward. And reading between the lines, he didn't want to get into details about the past, so closure didn't make sense.

"No, Mom, I don't."

She sighed groggily.

"Okay, sweetheart. Now I know how to reply to his mother. God always works it out. For you—and for Curtis."

Her sleepy and slow voice suddenly roused. "Hey, by the way, did you know he had another concussion?"

Vertigo set in as I recalled his aunt's warnings so long ago.

"What?"

My body froze. My mind seized one word and clung to it. *Concussion. Another head injury.* All my logical reasons for not contacting him vanished. I considered hanging up immediately and calling him, but before I could act, Mom continued.

"Corinne. Don't worry. It happened months ago. Skiing, I think. Apparently he had a challenging year, but he's much better now."

My heart called his name while my senses corralled my scattered emotions. Curtis was okay and I had no right or permission to allow my feelings to invade his life. I ended the call and went for a run.

An anorexic can go through periods of progress followed by steep declines. It's no surprise. The physical characteristics of a body can change rapidly, but the mental illness takes longer to address. All the right tools, the best intentions, the desire to recover are no match for the monster—unless there has been enough time to treat the psychiatric aspects of the disorder and get to its root of origin. For me, this spelled trouble.

During treatment, Susan asked me how many times a week I worked out. I told her three to four. I'd started lying again. Well, to be fair, she didn't specify what she meant by "worked out." To me a workout included a hard session of lifting in the gym. If I'd been completely honest, I would have added the two days I ran on the treadmill followed by the one I ran on the track—seven days total.

I thought my slight manipulation of the term could be forgiven. I thought Susan couldn't possibly understand how I felt about working out. Working out wasn't some compulsion I'd added when I started having eating issues. Back in middle school I'd wake up before dawn and go for a jog with my dad. I enjoyed waking up early. I enjoyed being with Dad. I also enjoyed running. When I entered high school, my purpose for exercise shifted from recreation to building a stronger, athletic body. Gym class became more competitive. The scales came out. We weighed publicly, compared privately. Lessons regarding a healthy diet warned against weighing too much. I don't recall concern about weighing too little. No, Susan was wrong. Working out wasn't the problem here.

Early November brought on a sudden increase in my workload: midterms, research papers, and sorority commitments, all culminating in the same week. I organized my time into what I thought were manageable chunks, working for a couple of hours, then de-stressing with exercise. I responded to pressure during times of increased stress with more intense workouts. I needed the endorphin rush and knew it would come from pushing myself through the pain of exertion. No pain, no gain.

Friday signaled the end of a long, hard week. An afternoon session at the gym kept my mind off reevaluating my academic performance. The alarm on the elliptical beeped. I looked up and realized I'd been running for an hour. Exhausted, I thought about what I'd eaten so far that day. Fat-free yogurt and an apple—*oh, and a banana.*

I should have quit, but my competitive nature drew me to the treadmill's touch screen. I adjusted the time for another thirty minutes and threw my workout towel over the digital readout. My legs stumbled. I kept running. Spots before my eyes finally caused me to stop. *Enough for today.* On the walk home, my legs felt heavy. My eyes burned when I blinked. I needed water.

Staggering through the doorway, I collapsed to the floor. I remember the coolness of the tiles as my mind drifted into a euphoric state. I must have dozed off because when I came to, I giggled, somewhat impressed that I'd pushed myself so hard. But as I tried to move, my limbs remained unresponsive. Confusion disoriented me. Had I hit my head?

There was no one home. No one to call out to. So I lay there, trapped in my own mind, trying to figure out how to get help. I'd left my phone in my room. That's where I had to go. I focused my thoughts and forced my body to move, to obey me.

My right arm and leg seemed more willing than the rest of my body, so I used what I could and inched my way across the living room floor. Progress proved difficult, impeded every few feet by a severe cramping in my calf. The effort to slide my arm down to the muscle was beyond my ability, and even if I had managed that feat, the strength required to massage the ache was nonexistent. Slight stretching and waiting for the spasms to ease off gave me a minute at each stop to fully appreciate the pounding in my head before I could continue slithering on toward my room. Finally, I reached my phone—thank God I'd place it on my rug next to my books.

Sabreena worked on campus when she didn't have class. I knew she'd come. I heard the door only minutes later. She ran into my room to find me sprawled out on my floor. She picked me up, laid me on my bed, and fetched a glass of water. When she came back, she looked concerned.

"Corinne, this has to stop."

Her angry undertone scared me. Sabreena knew I had issues with eating. She'd even made comments here and there about my weight, or lack of it. But she'd never been so direct and short.

"I know," I whispered. I promised her I'd stop working out for a while.

The slow and bumpy path to recovery irritated me. It seemed every time I determined to make a change, I'd build some momentum only to find myself once again pulled into the habitual rituals of my addiction. I'd kept my appointments with my nutritionist and had tried to adhere to her recommendations. I'd added foods and tried to stay positive. And now I'd agreed to drop my workouts. Discouraged, I wondered if I'd ever reach some summit where I could stand and say I'd overcome the monster within me.

I had more time to think once I stopped exercising. I wanted to investigate why I needed anorexia in my life in the first place. Maybe that was the only way to rid myself of it. I began by revisiting the recent conversation with my mother. It bothered me that I still thought about Curtis. I explained away the irritation as silly and childish, and that he was just one of the many people I prayed for. But something down deep in my soul prompted me to explore the idea further.

I'd grown up familiar with the power of prayer. I'd witnessed answers to prayer many times—even personally. Sometimes the answer was an over-the-top "yes," like my acceptance to Chapman. I also knew the destruction of a devastating "no"—"no" to my continued relationship with Curtis. But then I'd heard many testimonies about "no" answers leading to unimaginable blessings.

God didn't hate me. He wasn't mean. And He wasn't punishing me. I sensed Him waiting for me to fully trust Him. And He seemed to be waiting for something else. A question pulled at my heart. It pressed me, convicted me. I'd wondered if I was enough. Was I good enough? Just me, just as I was? I felt God pressing me with those same questions. Was He enough—for me? Just Him? Just as He was? My heart sank as I realized that I loved Him conditionally. I loved and trusted Him when He answered my calls the way I wanted. But what about the times I didn't care for the answers He gave? Would I—could I—love Him then?

During times of struggle, He had gently guided me through the pain. I didn't listen, or want to listen, to the whisper-call He'd placed in my core—not only to face my demons, but to help other girls face theirs. I began to realize the pain I'd experienced would not be wasted. He would take the pain, the trials, and the loss and use those things for good. I simply had to trust Him and rest in the process of it all.

I suddenly appreciated that God was maturing me, teaching me to look to Him for my security. In my horizontal perspective, I'd tried and failed to control how others saw me and whether they'd accept me and stay with me. But there was a call inside me to grasp the faith of my youth and to accept the One who'd always been there. He would heal me if I released all my worries to Him and allowed Him to take the lead.

As I thought about God and Curtis, I realized why I'd never given a name to my illness. People had asked why I didn't call it Ed—acronym for eating disorder—the name given by many who suffer with this affliction. Ed sounds like a guy's name and is supposed to personify an abusive boyfriend. Some people live with Ed. Others kick Ed to the curb after having reached their limit. Those in recovery sometimes talk about their journey breaking up with Ed.

I'd already had a boyfriend when my eating disorder began, and he wasn't abusive. He loved me. And besides, my sense of loyalty rejected the idea of some other "guy" overriding the loving words Curtis had implanted in my mind. I guess that's why my illness revealed itself as a monster to me and not as an Ed.

I also came to realize two key factors that greatly influenced my desire for recovery—motivation and love. For me, the motivation part came from Chapman. I'd do whatever it took to stay there. The love came from those around me—my parents, my friends, my sisters, and the love Curtis had for me so long ago. They'd reassured me every day how much they loved me. They didn't care about my B-student status or my bad days. They'd lifted me up and encouraged me in every way.

All this time in mindful reflection allowed me to accept my value in the universe: that I was created, loved, and cared for; that I had purpose; that I mattered; that my worth was permanent. And with those insights, I finally felt permission to engage the world around me, to seek out the life I was made for—but first I needed a dose of unconditional love in human form. Fortunately, I knew just where to get it.

Grandma Sweety

Everyone should have a Grandma Sweety. Mine turned ninety the fall of 2012. Her two daughters, along with her grandkids, planned a surprise party over Thanksgiving break, inviting relatives near and far to come celebrate the matriarch who held us all together. Mom had given me the task of escorting the birthday girl into a room where everyone yelled, "Surprise!" I wasn't sure if scaring a ninety-year-old woman by shouting out *surprise* had been the best decision, but then again, I know my grandma.

Grandma Sweety, my great-grandmother, is full of stories of a life well lived during a time of profound struggle. When her husband, my great-grandpa, ran off with another woman, she enrolled in nursing school at the age of forty-seven then bought a house on her own three years later. Her husband came back, but on her terms.

Her eldest son, my grandpa, died a year to the day before I was born. Despite this loss and many others,

Grandma Sweety has never stopped appreciating the life surrounding her. She giggles. She jokes. She's happy to hear from me whenever I call, even if that call is long overdue. There's never any guilt. I don't think I've ever detected disappointment in her voice, not even a phrase like, "I haven't heard from you in a while." She's the most present person I've ever met.

Grandma Sweety lives on her own as a widow, and she defies her age. She drives quite well. She takes out her trash. She enjoys visits from her brother and his wife who come by every Saturday evening after church; once in a while they find me there.

My favorite pastime with Grandma is to sit in her living room and throw pillows back and forth while watching the pop quartet Il Divo perform on TV. Sometimes I catch her glancing over at the four handsome men singing on the screen. You'd think their performance was a private concert for her alone given the way she acts. I love watching the childlike joy on her face as she listens.

Her home is my comfort. It gives me rest as I look around and ponder the stories behind the knick-knacks. Angels in all shapes and sizes hover on the mantle above her recliner. Dainty teacups with saucers decorate the cream-colored walls. Across the room, an organ adorned with cranberry-colored glass lamps invites memories of Corbin and me sitting on the instrument's oak bench and reaching for the row of pedals below it while belting out original versions of childhood classics.

"Grandma, what's your favorite possession?"

"Well, let me see. Why do you ask?"

She was working on a crossword puzzle attached to a clipboard on her lap.

"You have so many things. I don't know. Curious, I guess."

She paused before answering, "I guess I'd have to say a pair of heels I have." Then she squeaked and announced, "Twelve across!"

She filled in the answer on the crossword and added, "You know, Corinne, I'm not getting any younger. If there's something in this house you want, you'd better speak up. Your mom's already called the yellow quilt and the church pew."

I thought that was morbid.

"Grandma, why shoes?"

"You couldn't get shoes during the war. Shoes were hard to come by."

"So why those shoes?" I asked.

"I was on vacation with your grandpa and I fell—in those shoes. The heel broke off on one of them, and your grandpa had it fixed for me."

Grandma Sweety's shoe—the representation of a life of hardship. Her young prince had come to repair the brokenness. I'd been broken. My fairy tale life had turned into a pile of shards. But things were looking up. I was looking up, finding my healing from above. After considering all the sentiments attached to an object, I no longer thought of Mom's request as morbid; in fact, I now knew what I wanted from the house.

Grandma Sweety on her ninetieth birthday.

Something to Remind Me

After the visit with Grandma, I noticed a common theme in the lives of the survivors I'd met. They valued simple things like the taste of strawberries and cream, or the bond of a friendship bracelet, or even the attachment to an old pair of shoes. It made sense to me that those who'd endured hardship achieved an understanding—a level of thankfulness—not easily grasped by those who lacked experience with prolonged adversity or grief. Taking an opportunity to put a thankful spirit into practice, I spent the holidays with my family focusing on and counting my blessings.

At first the exercise took some effort, but by spring, I could see results of the mental training. Addressing the core issues had made all the difference. I'd added some healthy weight and finally maintained it. My heavy blanket of chronic exhaustion was cast aside. I found the feeling liberating. A golden brown hue coated my body as the shedding of my sweatshirt allowed the rays of the California sun to penetrate my exposed skin. My eyes were clear and rested. My muscles contracted with renewed power, crushing the abusive nature of my eating disorder.

Something else happened that spring. After a long and hard road of fighting against my nutritionist, I'd finally come to trust her. Susan's patience and persistence had kept me accountable until the emotional healing kicked in. Even when I'd lied, even when I'd called at the last minute to cancel an appointment, she never gave up on me. Looking back, I think she knew I wanted recovery.

One day in May, I sat across from Susan in her office, my hands placed calmly on my lap. A year before, my nails would have dug into the chair's arm, bracing myself for a reprimand. Each appointment with Susan had included a blind weigh-in to keep me from obsessing over a specific number. Susan would tell only if I'd lost or gained. If I'd lost weight, Susan would remind me of the benefits of recovery. If I'd gained, my monster would remind me of the dangers of putting on weight. One short year ago, no matter if I'd lost or gained, there would have been an argument in my head over who'd lied to whom.

How far had I come to reach a place where I didn't care about seeing a number on the scale? My mind drifted to the day I forcefully threw my beloved scale into the trash. That was months ago. I remember venturing out to the plastic tub several times to retrieve it, only to pause then force myself back inside the house. I could hear when the garbage truck finally arrived and lifted the bin. I imagined my most prized possession dumped onto a heap of items people didn't want.

These days Susan and I were more likely to discuss balance, coping skills, and variety in food choices now that my weight had stabilized. I looked forward to open and honest conversation, knowing my pulse would remain consistent and my mind clear throughout our visits.

Susan broke the silence by asking me, "Corinne, do you know what today is?"

The look on her face implied good news.

"It's Monday," I replied slyly, remembering how I hate Mondays.

Susan scanned a pile of papers on her lap. She flipped through them as if looking for something important. The suspense was paralyzing. My thoughts darted about. Had I reached some milestone? Was Susan going to say the time had come to stop seeing her? I didn't know if I was ready for that.

"Ah, yes. Here it is," Susan said, interrupting my thoughts. "It's been two years, Corinne. Two years ago today."

It took me a minute to catch up. I hadn't been at Chapman for two years. I hadn't even known Susan for two years. Then I got it. It had been two years since my first visit to get help for my "orthorexia" only to have it renamed for the monster it really was. Two years since I'd been jolted by the label *anorexic*. Two years since I'd begun a battle I became determined to win. Susan continued by saying I was doing well in recovery.

My jaw dropped and I braced my forehead with my hands. Staring at the floor, I caught a glimpse of a single tear dropping onto the carpet.

There were times I thought that phrase would never be said to me or about me: "Doing well in recovery." Sure, in my mind, I strived for recovery, I longed for recovery, my goal was recovery. I saw that term as some grandiose concept off in the distance and just out of reach. And yet, now I was being referred to as progressing "in my recovery." There had been so much pain, growth, and determination to change what had come to define me. I had been the anorexic girl. Now, my identity was changing into a girl in recovery. I had fought, and fought hard for that. I knew I still had a long way to go and a lot more work to do, but at least I'd reached a point where I knew I was over a hump. I'd never go back to where I was two years ago. I'd never go back to where I was one year ago. I was making progress and that alone was good enough. I, was good enough.

Dazed, I left the room, but I wasn't alone. People who helped me through my struggles as an outpatient accompanied me in my thoughts as I descended the stairs and exited the building.

Delaney, my mentor and big sis, who made me face my fears.

Sabreena, who on so many occasions allowed me to climb into her bed and to snuggle when feeling cold or sad and who helped me fight abusive self-talk.

Christine, my grand big sis in the sorority, who kept me grounded as my mind raced with lies and deceit.

Grace, the gorgeous blonde who warned me about the seriousness of this illness and who challenged me to get better.

Michael, the guy I'd dated for nine months, who made me laugh and taught me not to take myself so seriously.

Sophe, the girl I'd met in Colorado before school started, who helped me through that horrific first semester.

And of course Curtis, my first love, who taught me what dreams are made of and who showed me that someone could love me for just being me.

More people came to mind who had helped me along the way. They'd made a difference in my life, allowing me at last to accept the words Susan had said.

I opened the door to my car and stood thinking about my journey. I decided I wanted something permanent as a remembrance and a reminder. It would be something to honor the people who had believed in me when I hadn't believed in myself. I wanted a mark of freedom.

Needles had never interested me. Marking myself seemed unnatural. That said, the idea of a particular tattoo, the symbol for recovery on the website for the National Eating Disorders Association, lingered in the back of my mind. The site's logo has two unconnected lines that form a heart shape. Next to the logo are the words "Feeding hope." Recovery. Feeding. Hope. These words had become central to my concept of healing.

I decided that this tattoo would be a way of remembering my struggle out of a dismal place. But it took the milestone of hearing I was actually in recovery in order for me to feel I'd earned the right to wear the symbol. For me, the tattoo had to represent a turning point. It was permanent, and the decision not to go back to losing weight or to yield to a disease controlling my thoughts had to be permanent too. If I got the tattoo, I'd have to assume the responsibility of staying well.

"Mom," I started cautiously, "I have something to tell you."

"Sure, honey. I'm listening."

"I wanna get a tattoo."

The proclamation had rushed out of my mouth and formed one giant nonsensical phrase. Then ...

dead silence at the other end of the line. I could only imagine her disapproval—my poor mother, turning pale, shaking her head as if to say, "Who is this? Where has my daughter gone?"

Pacing the bedroom floor, I continued my side of what would surely become an argument. I had to regurgitate the thoughts I had processed before she could cut me off, before I could chicken out.

"Mom, I need this. I want this. The tattoo is something that will remind me of where I've been, how far I've come, and who I am now—not who I was then." I had to convince her.

I became adamant, passionately defending my reasoning. "I *am* doing this. I don't need your approval, but I want your blessing."

Did I really say that? I could get in a lot of trouble. I have so much respect for my mother. She's my best friend but also a mentor and a leader in my life. I was entering dangerous waters by informing her of my intentions rather than asking for permission.

Silence again fell over the line. My palms moist with sweat, I clutched the phone in a death grip—hoping, praying the scolding wouldn't be too extreme. Then she spoke.

"Honey, you've come such a long way and I'm so very proud of you. Sounds like you've thought about this and what it means to you. Can you send me a picture after you get it?"

My knees weakened. I had to sit down to keep from falling. The importance of a mother's approval and support cannot be underestimated, especially when an idea goes against her own beliefs.

A burly guy told me to sit down in a red reclining chair. My heart dove into the pit of my stomach, sending acid up into my throat, burning the sides with grim anticipation. Members of my cheering section— Sabreena, my roommate, and Karinne, my new little sister in Gamma Phi who shares a version of my name—stood behind a thick, yellow strip of barrier tape along the floor. According to a recent law, no one but the tattoo artist could be close to a customer during a procedure. (I imagined some delusional idiot holding a needle and inking someone to death.) The girls each held up their iPhones, recording my every move.

My eyes were closed, but my ears could make out the sounds of tools being assembled on the work tray. My fear of needles beckoned me to run. I pictured a Frankenstein moment with a mad scientist at his station of pain. Still, I couldn't help but want to peek from behind the heavy draperies that were my eyelids to witness this insanity. Before I'd come, I'd promised myself I wouldn't look, but now I couldn't decide which was stronger—my fear or my desire not to miss one second of this monumental event.

My friend Sabreena has many tattoos representing landmarks in her life. She'd warned me not to take any strong medication beforehand—not because she wanted me to feel pain but because she wanted me to remember the sensation.

"You need to feel it. You need to experience the pain. I cannot describe to you how it feels. It will hurt, but if you are serious about getting a tattoo, you need to experience all of it, and not just the outcome."

I opened my eyes and became aware of the surrounding details. Latex gloves, a bandage, a bottle of ink, the needle—all real and all about to affect me.

The tattoo artist, a big Samoan man, placed a dark stencil on the right side of my right wrist. I decided to put the recovery symbol on the underside of my wrist—not too obvious, but recognizable to a knowing eye. The mark is unmistakable to many who have suffered long and hard with this disease. When he lifted the stenciled paper, which ironically reminded me of a baking sheet used for making cookies, the black, heart-shaped symbol remained imprinted on my skin.

The long side of the symbol's heart reminds me of what I used to be: a walking skeleton, a dead person among the living. The shorter, rounder part of the heart completes my journey, reminding me to love my body and to keep striving in recovery.

A loud buzzing began to fill my ears. I sprang to attention. Shots of panic darted through my nervous system as the sound of swarming killer bees came straight at me.

"You ready?" the tattoo artist asked. It was more of a statement than a question.

I couldn't take my eyes off of the tool about to pierce my skin, but I silently nodded. The buzzing began again. The machine inched closer and closer to my perfectly untouched skin. *Do I really want to do this?* Suddenly, he balked.

"Stop it!" he commanded.

"What?" I asked, a little perturbed. Here I sat, ready to go, and he was bailing right before contact? Who would do that?

"You're holding your breath. If you hold your breath, you're gonna pass out," he chided.

Now my frustration turned inward. *Stay calm and breathe!*

"Okay, I'm sorry. I'll try my best," I said, my voice trembling.

Sabreena and Karinne started to make bets behind the boundary line.

"I'll give her five minutes before she needs to take a break," Sabreena said.

"I'll give her two," Karinne wagered.

Their comments replaced my fear with determination.

"Let's do this," I said to no one in particular.

I winced in agony at the oncoming feeling and at the idea of facing my needle phobia head-on. At first contact the sensation bordered on fire ants gnawing at my skin accompanied by bee stings down my wrist. Although it was piercing, the pain was also pleasurable in a weird way, replacing previous sorrows with a symbol of the future. I'd earned this, and after the first sixty seconds passed, the penetrations became bearable. I opened my eyes and began to watch as ink sank into my skin.

"Do you need a break?" the Samoan asked, noticing my free hand gripping the side of the chair.

"No. Keep going," I said, intent on proving my friends wrong. I'm stronger than I look, especially when someone tells me I can't do something.

"There. You're done," he said.

"Seriously? That didn't take more than fifteen minutes," I replied.

As the artist cleaned away the excess ink, I looked at my friends. My future, and my promise to myself and to others that I'd never return to the destructive habits of my past, were now plainly visible for all to see.

"So what does this mean exactly?" the tattoo artist asked as he applied ointment to the slightly bloodied area.

"It's the anorexia recovery symbol," I said with gratitude and delight.

His eyes met mine. "Wow, good for you! It may not look like it, but I'm actually a recovered bulimic."

The compassion in his voice and the empathy in his gaze led me to believe him without question. I sat there, astonished. I'd judged this man before I knew him, but his revelation turned the tattoo experience into a valuable lesson. I learned that eating disorders couldn't be classified according to race, gender, age, or weight. This big, burly guy represented a brother in suffering—a survivor like me. How appropriate that he branded my body with a healing mark. With my growing awareness of the prevalence of eating disorders, my tattoo began to stand for more than just me.

My resolve to maintain a healthy mind and body was soon tested as my boyfriend of nine months showed up on my patio two weeks before Spring Formal and gave me that look. My yellow chiffon gown with jewel-encrusted, heart-shaped bodice had just arrived in the mail. It rested on the entry table as Michael made his way to my room.

"I can't do this anymore," he said, his eyes avoiding mine.

I stood there quietly and considered his presence in my bedroom for what would be the last time. As

I looked at him, my thumb fidgeted for my missing purity ring.

"It had to end sooner or later," I said, resigning myself to the inevitable.

He gave me one last hug. My body went numb.

"I'm sorry," he whispered.

Michael turned and slowly departed, taking my boyfriend and best friend all in one go. I was thankful that he'd done it in person, though, and that I didn't have to wonder why. That last month we'd had a series of arguments over nothing that mattered—that slow separation until someone finally made the call. It had to be him. I rarely gave up on anything, even when I should.

Delaney consoled me on the couch. Sometime later she summed up my relationship with Michael by saying, "Are you really that surprised? If you were a wind-up doll and I pulled your string, it would say, 'What the heck did I do?'"

She was right. He preferred his space, especially when sick or mad. I thrived on care giving and required conversation during an argument—that communication thing again. The main reason for the breakup? "Corinne, you're too nice," my friends informed me.

The end of the relationship plus the added stress of finals should have triggered old habits of restricting. But when my monster came with its usual temptations, the voice sounded more irritating than threatening. I answered my monster by joining my friends for tailgating at an Angels baseball game. I refused to look back over my past and didn't overly mourn the present. I ate a burger instead—the whole mouthwatering burger.

I was sad, yes, but not broken. Not this time. I counted on the fact that God had plans waiting for me. But I still had a beautiful gown and no date. So who saved the day? My brother. Corbin flew to Los Angeles and took me to my formal, regaining the title he'd held on the playground of our youth: my hero. We laughed and danced and talked for hours on a yacht under a picture-perfect Southern California night sky.

The following day I received a gift—a book titled *Why Men Love Bitches: From Doormat to Dreamgirl.* I laughed when I opened it and contemplated myself as a bitch. Might as well let a toddler run in a china shop. It just wouldn't look right. I preferred to remain nice.

Some people find this part of my character—being too nice—annoying. Some think it's useful for target practice. Others maintain it's a weakness. I'm okay with that now. I can't be liked by everyone, but I can be liked by some, and those are the people I put my energy into. I can no longer afford to obsess over the thoughts and motivations of others. Accepting who I am can deliver a major blow to a disease that lives on accusing and putting down its host.

Peanut Butter

In the summer before my junior year, I entered a new phase in recovery. I'd faced triggers without backsliding. I'd disarmed the guilt that followed a meal by using positive self-talk. I'd given up worrying so much and had accepted the idea that everybody has challenges. Now, I was working on the necessary skills to face the problems that life guaranteed with its ups and downs.

The lease ended on our house close to Chapman, so Delaney and I decided to move into a bigger place with another Gamma Phi sister. I'd have a longer commute to campus, but the rental had two stories and a nice side yard. I'd no longer have the option to eat in the safety of the cafeteria, but Trader Joe's down the street sold pre-packaged meals—and the checkout aisles did not include magazines!

However, while I'd made tremendous progress in recovery, some foods still troubled me: quesadillas, ice cream, pasta, pizza, burgers, avocados—and peanut butter. Even though I had tried these foods in my recovery phase, I had yet to realize a happy medium between a normal healthy diet, treats, and foods I just preferred not to have. Mom said I didn't have to include all foods in my diet just to prove I no longer restricted.

I contemplated the idea of eating peanut butter. Should I have a goal of eating peanut butter on a regular basis, or should I count it as a treat? Did I want it at all? My mouth would salivate just thinking about it. But was it the taste I yearned for, or the memory of the peanut-butter-and-honey sandwiches my mother made for me as a kid?

One day I decided to be spontaneous. I drove to the grocery store, headstrong and rebellious. On a mission for peanut butter, I marched through the entrance, reminding myself that lots of people ate all kinds of foods and lived to see another day. I would not blow up. I could eat what was really only ground-up nuts and be fine. But when I reached the aisle with the peanut butter, my monster told me to walk away, or else. Or else what? We'd been through this before with less offensive items, so I knew the drill. If I didn't buy the peanut butter, something I wanted to do on my own initiative without encouragement or help from anyone else, I'd be feeding my monster. My stubborn disposition wouldn't allow for backsliding.

I approached the peanut butter selections, picked up a jar, and placed it in my cart, then immediately retrieved it. I couldn't help myself; I had to look at the back of the label. There were 190 calories in two tablespoons. Sixteen grams of fat. *Woah, that's a lot.* I put the jar back on the shelf and looked at the other options one after another until I realized they all contained about the same calorie and fat content. *Maybe I could eat a tiny portion on a spoon.* My eating disorder screamed its disapproval, but I told myself my monster wasn't the boss of me anymore. I placed the jar back in my basket and quickly distracted my thoughts with other items on my list, foods that ranked higher in comfort for me: yogurt, fruit, and packaged salads with small toppings of cheese and chicken.

The checkout line sparked a temper tantrum inside my head. The voice kept yelling at me to put the peanut butter back. I'd had enough. The thing had irritated me to a point where I wanted it out of my life. *Just go! Gosh!* I mentally shut a door on the monster and zoned out. I needed to do what I'd set out to do— buy the peanut butter—and get home.

Unpacking the bags of groceries, I grabbed the peanut butter jar and moved it to the edge of the counter. I crouched down to inspect its label. *I can't believe I bought this.* I focused in on the protein information. *Eight grams. Protein builds muscle. Strong muscle equals strong heart. Strong beating heart equals life. Life equals winning.*

"You bought peanut butter?" Delaney screeched. She trotted over, excited that I had purchased something unconventional for my shelf in the kitchen. I hadn't seen her when I'd walked in or I would have been more discreet.

"Yeah, I did," I confessed in a hushed voice.

"What's the problem?" she asked.

Delaney knew me.

"I'm scared. This is a big step for me, buying it on my own. It contains a lot of fat."

Delaney laughed. "I know, but you're much stronger than that. And besides, this is a good fat!"

She paused, then said, "I have an idea."

Delaney disappeared into the living room and came back with a permanent marker. She grabbed the jar from the counter and blacked out the nutritional information before I could stop her.

"There. All better!" she said.

I looked at the black streak covering my skepticism. I wasn't angry. The old me would have reacted. The old me would have walked away. Now an overwhelming sense of appreciation lifted a weight from my shoulders, and it happened with the stroke of a small black marker. Delaney smiled at me. She reached for two spoons. Standing in the kitchen, we playfully licked the peanut butter off of the spoons, and I smiled. My monster was nowhere around.

My Sanctuary

D's efforts accomplished three things: 1) reminded me of the value of connection, 2) gave my mind a nudge over a bump, and 3) shed light once again on one of the reasons I'd become sick—my tendency to obsess over things. Lesson learned. God had clearly arranged the perfect big sis for me.

My phone buzzed in my purse. A text read, "Hi, Corinne. This is Anni, one of your sorority sisters. I was wondering if we could meet for coffee."

The crisp fall air blew against my skin, but I wasn't cold. My hair was longer, fuller, soft to the touch, and colored brown—a change representing the new me. The nerves in my arms twitched from my workout. I felt my biceps and appreciated their strength and their shape. Junior year was off to a great start.

Anni and I met at Jazzman's. I ordered a chai latte, and she, a tall black. I started the conversation.

"I've seen you around. Our sorority is so big. It's hard to get to know everyone. What's your major?"

She appeared preoccupied. I wondered if she even heard my question.

"Gamma Phi is big. I know you, though. You look a lot different than you did last year. I heard you were sick. Anorexia, right? Did you have anorexia? Sorry if I'm being so blunt."

"No, no. It's fine. I'm actually in recovery. I'm much better now."

I noticed her foot tapping the ground, her fingers fiddling with her napkin.

"Corinne ..." Anni started to speak but paused to take a deep breath before continuing. "I've got it. I've had it for a while now. Months. I'm scared and I don't know what to do."

She began talking faster.

"My parents don't know, and I'm losing weight. I can't stop it. What do you think I should do?" Then she looked at me, and I could tell she regretted what she'd said.

"Please don't tell anyone," she said cautiously.

I grabbed her hand and reassured her I wouldn't.

"Is it true you did it without going in-house?" she asked.

I felt an instant bond and understood her pain, her silent suffering. I squeezed her hand slightly and held her gaze.

"Anni, I have to ask you some questions. Three, to be exact. But you have to be completely honest with me. Okay? Nothing will matter here today unless you can search yourself and be completely honest. Do you think you can do that?"

Anni nodded but looked down. I knew it would be hard for her to hear, much less act on, what I was about to tell her.

"Okay. First and most important, do you want to get better? Don't answer me too quickly. Think about it and be honest. If you don't want to get well, no person and no program can help you."

"Corinne, I'm tired."

She looked up at me and then out of the window.

"I'm so tired. I think about this every day, all day. I'm getting sicker and I'm not sure if I'll ever be okay."

She looked back at me generally and then into my eyes. "But yes, I want to get better."

Her answer encouraged me.

"Good," I said. "Second question. Do you have a support system? People who can come alongside you and love you and be there for you no matter what?"

"No one knows. Not my parents. Not my friends. No one."

I considered her thin frame and thought that the people closest to her must know something. And if they didn't know, I was pretty sure they had their suspicions. Anorexics become quite skilled at hiding their sickness, but they aren't perfect. Mistakes are made along the way, and those mistakes leave a trail of questions. It's just that no one knows how to ask them.

"Anni, you've got to tell your parents. I'm sure they would want to know. I have an amazing nutritionist. I can give you her number. It takes a team. I have a nutritionist and a psychologist I see once a week, and I've done this for two years."

Her tone softened. "I think my parents would help, but I'm scared to tell them and I don't want to leave Chapman."

"Anni, you know what this disease can do. It destroys everything you care about while slowly destroying you. It's a death sentence if you stay where you are. You could lose Chapman, your friends, your family—your life. I know this. People got sick of dealing with my disease. My family went through so much pain. It changed me, Anni. Don't wait. I'm telling you. Do not wait."

"What's the third question?" she asked.

I paused a moment and peered deep into her hollowed eyes, trying to gain access around the defensive boundaries of her captor.

"Are you ready for the fight of your life?" I asked calmly and deliberately, allowing the words to settle before I continued.

"There's a reason you got here. You have to fight the illness first. Then you have to look at the underlying issues that triggered it. I can tell you my story sometime, but yours will be different from mine, so your path to healing will also be different. All I can do is point you in the right direction and be here for you. I won't tell anyone. That's up to you. But I will be here and support you. You can do this, Anni. I'll be checking on you. But you have to be ready. Are you ready?"

"I have to be ready, don't I?" she replied.

We paused and sipped our drinks to back off the severity of the topic. She smiled then attempted to lighten the mood.

"What's your major anyway? Are you in film?"

"No, that's not my passion. I'm majoring in health communications. I want to help girls like us."

After that meeting, I needed to clear my head. I jumped into my car and headed down the 55 toward Crystal Cove. It promised to be a gorgeous day. Passing by the John Wayne Airport, I turned up the radio then veered onto the 73. A plane passed low overhead. The image of a furry mascot decorated its tail wing. *Is that a bobcat or …?* Tilting my head and searching my mind for a match, I retrieved something unexpected—a memory. I breathed in slow and deep, accepting the warmth and comfort of restoration. I exhaled, and smiled. I'd waited a long time for this. I was still driving, but my mind occupied another time and space.

Hauling heavy heart and bag through the Denver International Airport, Mom had abruptly stopped at the end of a long line of disgruntled passengers receiving word that our canceled flight would leave the same time the following day. Apparently our plane required some TLC. Me too. A little over an hour earlier, I'd stood on Curtis' lawn, absorbing his smell, his touch, his kiss for what would have to last me a good three months until I saw him again.

I couldn't believe our luck. I dialed his number, my hands shaking with excitement.

"Curtis, you're not going to believe this."

I'm sure I looked like the odd one out in a sea of complaining protesters as I told Curtis about our good fortune. But for me, the universe had shined its favor upon us once again, granting two star-crossed sixteen-year-old sweethearts the most precious gift of time. Curtis dropped his plans for the day and night and met me at my uncle's house in Castle Rock, a fifty-five-minute drive from the airport. The news said the night sky would host an unusual display, an impressive meteor shower. We couldn't be bothered, giggling and enraptured as we explored newly hatched inside jokes in the privacy of my uncle's basement.

Laughing to myself over the recollection, I realized I'd finally made peace with the past. I'd also settled on the best gift I could give Curtis in return for all he'd done for me. I began praying for God to give my first love an abundant life. I asked that He bring Curtis love, laughter, peace, and health and that He be bigger than Curtis ever imagined. I released all my bitterness, anger, sorrow, grief, and loss and replaced them with hope, joy, healing, and love remembered.

Pulling into the familiar lot, I put the memory on hold and parked my car. The smell of earth and salt saturated the air. A light breeze refreshed my spirit and welcomed me into my sanctuary. Venturing along my regular route, I passed the occasional cottontail rabbit among the desert plants. The moment was filled with suspense. It excited me a little to speculate about my special spot. Would it be the same as I left it? I rounded a bend and took in the view. Same waves. Same rocks. Same tide pools. Just as I remembered.

I descended a steep incline to the beach where I sat and thought about the significance of this place: my brother and me searching for tiny sea creatures in these tide pools on family vacations; the rock where I'd sat and prayed when I first visited Chapman. I was happy then. I was happy now. There were no regrets. Not one.

My thoughts then wandered to my mom. She'd apologized to me for so many things. I could tell she carried guilt for not recognizing sooner the seriousness of my illness. She wished she had enforced stricter boundaries regarding my relationship with Curtis. She felt her bad decisions exposed me to more pain than if she'd said no more often.

I looked out over the ocean with its risks and its beauty and realized you can't have one without the other. I loved her for allowing the risk—the long shot. There was beauty in that. Mom is a dreamer, like me. She believed in the possibility that two people had been brought together and had found a love that doesn't come along often. There could be no fault in that. I believe that God's a dreamer too. And He has a purpose in fulfilling them. God brought Curtis and me together in His perfect timing to learn about love. And indeed, I'd learned so much about love, not only from Curtis, but also from a God who loved me enough to give me a rare and extravagant gift when I needed it most.

And when the gift was gone, God captured every moment of pain and transformed the trials into overflowing blessings. He called me back to faith when loss and grief and lack of closure left me with nowhere to turn. And in that exercise alone, my reasoning gave way to hope in a future I do not yet know.

So what now? Our family has healed. Mom and I chat about decorating my apartment and the upcoming football season. Daddy is still my Atticus Finch, and Corbin, my best friend and my hero. (And good news: he covered his old tattoo with a much-improved Singapore skyline.)

I've wrestled with death—my monster, my weaker self—and have clawed my way back to renewed life. I know what it means to strive and to persevere when the world tells you you're not thin enough, not smart enough, not strong enough. I am one voice of hope proclaiming better days ahead. And no, I would not have chosen my path, but I now see the lessons and the growth that came from the struggle.

What about the future and that uncertainty that kept my mind spinning? I'm not so worried about that anymore. I know that I have a lot more to accomplish in this life, and if I can help a struggling girl (or boy) through their pain, my story is worth it.

There are many of us out there, suffering. We're in the "almost" category. Almost committed to in-house care. Almost battling heart conditions. Almost suicidal. Almost sick enough to be visible, to tell our stories. You may not see our pain; we conceal it well. But we are screaming inside, in our minds—where the monster waits.

My brother and me in 2013.

Epilogue

It's been more than a year since I finished this book. I'm not going to tell you I don't struggle. I do. But I haven't gone back. Not to the depths of the darkness that controlled me. I can choose not to now. And though I've come to accept that anorexia may always be with me, I'm not afraid of it. It no longer has a hold on me.

I continue to check myself, making sure I eat balanced meals of protein, carbs, veggies, and fats. I also push myself regularly to try something new or to eat something I want. Slowing down and savoring the foods are my next goals.

I have a supportive network of family and friends who keep me accountable and ask how I'm doing. I know what they mean when they ask.

Today I can say I'm wide-awake and happy with where I am in my life. I am able to look in the mirror and believe that I am beautiful in my own skin.

Corbin and I are closer than ever. Sometimes we revisit the past, but when we do, it's with gratitude for the journey.

I still visit my Grandma Sweetie. Together we make Blue Bell Homemade Vanilla shakes while listening to Il Divo on TV.

After graduating from Chapman, D moved to Arizona to work for her father. She continues to be my guardian and big sis.

Curtis has been amazing in his support of this book. We've communicated a bit by e-mail since last summer. At times it's somewhat awkward, but together, we've come to accept the past and have moved on with our lives in different directions.

Zazzy spent a year at Oxford. She soaked up all things British and all things Kate. I'm sure her life will be everything she's always dreamed of.

The roommates I had have all moved on. They've passed the Panther baton to me, and as I finish my senior year, they are with me.

In my mind, all who shaped my life walk with me and visit me—my family, my friends, those I have loved. There is no bitterness. There is only freedom.

Appendix

- 20 million women and 10 million men in the United States suffer at some point in their lives from a clinically significant eating disorder (Wade, Keski-Rahkonen, & Hudson, 2011).
- Anorexia has the highest fatality rate of any mental illness (Arcelus, J., Mitchell, A.J., Wales, J., & Nielson, S, 2011).
- Anorexia is the third-most common chronic illness among adolescents (Public Health Services Office, 2003).
- Those who suffer with eating disorders are 4 times more likely to abuse alcohol or other substances (Harrop&Marlatt, 2010).
- Twenty percent of people suffering from anorexia will prematurely die from complications related to this eating disorder, including suicide and heart problems (The Renfrew Center Foundation for Eating Disorders, 2003).

The *American Journal of Psychiatry* refers to anorexia as a well-ingrained maladaptive habit, and therefore early intervention is critical.

A Word about Statistics and the Media

As soon as statistics are published, they are outdated. I could refer to well-known statistics about the influence of print ads among other media, but in this fast-paced world of Twitter, Instagram, Facebook, and Snap-Chat, the numbers and means of influence would have changed by the time you read them.

What is unchanging? No one will deny eating disorders are on the rise. Whether in the United States, in Asia, or worldwide, the pressures to measure up—to be successful and beautiful—are more apparent and pervasive than ever before. Kids as young as 6 are being diagnosed with eating disorders. What are they looking for? What was I looking for? To be heard. To be successful. To have choices. As these elements decrease, the search for significance can sometimes lead to addiction. And there are people out there who offer community and support (both above and underground) in sites that encourage the addictive behavior, or the lifestyle, or however one chooses to refer to it. I will not list those sites here, generally or specifically. If you're already engrained in an eating disorder, you already know. You know the sites, the signals, the color of bracelet to wear on which wrist. And as soon as word is out, the site will change, the signal will change, but the underlying reasons remain. If we lose our voice, if we lose our perceived capacity to succeed, if we feel we can never measure up to the expectations placed on us (internally or externally), if we believe we are not heard … our success and identity may be found in the irony of striving for the lowest number on the scale.

Media must change. Body image, what is portrayed as beautiful, how we measure success must change. The life at risk could be that of your own daughter/ your own son/your wife/your friend. Help make the change.

Arcelus, J., Mitchell, A.J., Wales, J., & Nielson, S. (2011). Mortality rates in patients with Anorexia Nervosa and other eating disorders. Archives of General Psychiatry, 68(7), 724-731.

Harrop, E.N., & Marlatt, G. A. (2010). The comorbidity of substance use disorders and eating disorders in women: prevalence, etiology, and treatment. Addictive Behaviors, 35, 392-398.

Public Health Service's Office in Women's Health, Eating Disorder Information Sheet, 2000.

The Renfrew Center Foundation for Eating Disorders, "Eating Disorders 101 Guide: A Summary of Issues, Statistics and Resources," published September 2002, revised October 2003, http://www.renfrew.org.

Wade, T.D., Keski-Rahkonen A., & Hudson J. (2011). Epidemiology of eating disorders. In M. Tsuang and M. Tohen (Eds.), Textbook in Psychiatric Epidemiology (3rd ed.) (pp. 343–360). New York: Wiley.

Steps toward Recovery

Awareness: Some people refer to eating disorders as a lifestyle. Anorexia likes to hide under many masks. It is a lifestyle inasmuch as drug addiction or depression is a "lifestyle." The first step toward recovery is to understand that anorexia is a mental illness and should be treated as such by the sufferer, the health care providers, and those in charge of making/amending health care policy. A stranger came up to me early on in my disease and called me out on it, asking if I was okay. I denied I had a problem, but her comments and concern were planted along with many other seeds that led me toward awareness. Plant a seed in someone's life. Asking if someone's okay, or even offering someone a smile, may someday bring about change.

Desire: You have to want healing. I got to a place where I was tired of the thoughts harassing and controlling me. I knew I was on a path that would only grow darker if I didn't make a change. I had to want to get better before treatment could work.

Motivation: Find a reason to heal. At one time Chapman ranked higher in importance to me than anorexia. The thought of losing something I wanted motivated me to get help.

Support: I had great friends and family encouraging me every step of the way. The combination of a nutritionist and a psychologist helped me see that recovery might be possible.

Commitment: The will to fight and to keep fighting is critical for recovery. Triggers still come around, tempting me to fall back into unhealthy habits. But we all face struggles in life, and this is mine. However, I will press on one day at a time, knowing each day in recovery is a day I've won the fight.

Faith: I wouldn't have a story to tell and hope that there are better days ahead without faith. Someone watched over me and gave me hope for life on the other side of the pain. For me, that faith comes from a merciful God who reaches out, meets me where I'm at, and loves me unconditionally. And He is worthy of my trust.

My story is only one from among many survivors of eating disorders. Their journeys are different from mine. So are their paths to recovery. Some need in-house care and some do not. The National Eating Disorders Association website is the go-to place for information and help: www.nationaleatingdisorders.org.

Get informed. Get help. Never give up; never quit. Know there is hope.

CPSIA information can be obtained at www.ICGtesting.com
Printed in the USA
BVOW07s2013130515

400293BV00002B/2/P